SPECIALIZED JUSTICE

Specialized Justice

Courts, Administrative Tribunals, and a Cross-National Theory of Specialization

Stephen H. Legomsky

CLARENDON PRESS · OXFORD
1990

This book has been printed digitally and produced in a standard design in order to ensure its continuing availability

OXFORD
UNIVERSITY PRESS

Great Clarendon Street, Oxford OX2 6DP

Oxford University Press is a department of the University of Oxford.
It furthers the University's objective of excellence in research, scholarship, and education by publishing worldwide in

Oxford New York

Athens Auckland Bangkok Bogotá Buenos Aires Cape Town
Chennai Dar es Salaam Delhi Florence Hong Kong Istanbul Karachi
Kolkata Kuala Lumpur Madrid Melbourne Mexico City Mumbai Nairobi
Paris São Paulo Shanghai Singapore Taipei Tokyo Toronto Warsaw

with associated companies in Berlin Ibadan

Oxford is a registered trade mark of Oxford University Press in the UK and in certain other countries

Published in the United States by Oxford University Press Inc., New York

Reprinted 2001

ISBN 0-19-825429-6

To Lorraine,
Katie, and Annie

Acknowledgements

There are many to whom I owe a great deal. I thank the Washington University School of Law for the sabbatical leave that made this project possible. I am especially grateful to the Law Faculty of Victoria University of Wellington for receiving me as a Visiting Professor during the course of this study. The extraordinary kindness and hospitality of that faculty left my family and me with indelibly fond memories of New Zealand, many new friends to whom we feel particularly close, and an overwhelming desire to return. We felt privileged to have known Richard Kiwanuka, a wonderful friend whose premature death brought profound sadness to us and to countless others.

I record my deep appreciation to the many individuals who liberally shared their time and thoughts. They include the Rt. Hon. Geoffrey Palmer, the Prime Minister of New Zealand; the Rt. Hon. Sir Ronald Davison, the then Chief Justice; the Rt. Hon. Sir Robin Cooke, the President of the Court of Appeal; the Hon. Mr. Justice Chilwell, the Hon. Mr Justice Jeffries, the Hon. Mr Justice Holland, the Hon. Mr Justice Greig, the Hon. Mr Justice Tompkins, the Hon. Mr Justice Doogue; Professor Gordon Orr, Member, Waitangi Tribunal; Sir Kenneth Keith, Deputy President, Law Commission; and Mr Bill Mansfield, Deputy Secretary of the Department of Justice. I am especially grateful to High Court Deputy Registrar David Mangos, to Ms Ellen France, in the Office of the Deputy Prime Minister, and to Victoria University of Wellington Law Librarian Heather Toebes, for their extensive assistance. In the United States, the comments of Professors Walter Gellhorn and Ron Levin, Mr Jeff Lubbers, and Professors Dinah Shelton and Tom Sullivan were all invaluable. My secretary, Mary Ellen Powers, typed the entire manuscript with her own exceptional brand of skill, dedication, and warmth.

St Louis
October 1989

Contents

Table of Cases

NEW ZEALAND

UNITED KINGDOM

UNITED STATES

Table of Statutes and Regulations

Introduction: Specialized Justice

Life is more complicated than it used to be. The exponential growth of human knowledge has brought with it a degree of intricacy that dwarfs anything experienced in former times. For even the most talented individual to master even a single broadly defined field has become nearly impossible.

To cope with this heightened complexity, we have turned increasingly to the specialist and the subspecialist. Physicians specialize as ophthalmologists, who subspecialize in diseases of the retina. Chemical engineers subspecialize as environmental consultants, who further subspecialize as water pollution experts, who subspecialize still further in specific effluents.

The law is not immune from these forces. As new social problems emerge, and as society becomes aware of old social problems previously neglected, those who shape policy inevitably seek solutions in the law. The results are more legislation, more regulations, more case-law. The end-product is both large enough and complex enough to create a continually expanding need for legal specialists. The definitions of the specialities become progressively more esoteric.

One can applaud or condemn the increased breadth of the law and the specialization that it has engendered. But, whatever one's normative reaction, specialization within the field of law is a fact—for the present and for the foreseeable future. Specialist bar organizations mushroom. General associations of lawyers continue to sprout new sections. Legal academics specialize in their teaching and in their writing. Specialized government agencies, private industry, and other special interest groups invariably mean specialized legal staffs.

In recent years, this tide of increased reliance on specialist advocates has been attended by another phenomenon that has subtly begun to transform the dispensation of justice in fundamental ways: more frequent use of specialized adjudicators. The clearest examples of specialized adjudication have been at the administrative agency level. The importance of those specialized administrative bodies that perform adjudicative functions cannot today be doubted. In the United States, they are complemented by various article I 'courts' that are difficult to distinguish analytically from administrative tribunals.[1] Specialization has taken root as well in the article III courts.[2]

Resort to specialist adjudicators is not a uniquely American trend. Others have catalogued the roles of the numerous and diverse specialized tribunals in the Commonwealth countries.[3] In many of the Commonwealth countries, specialized courts or divisions of courts have also recently been created.[4] And in France and other European nations, a separate system of tribunals and courts has long been in place for the adjudication of administrative law disputes.[5]

[1] Examples include the bankruptcy courts, 28 USC §§ 151–8, the Court of Military Appeals, 10 USC § 867, the United States Tax Court, 26 USC §§ 7441–8, the Claims Court, 28 USC §§ 2501–22, and the United States Court of Veterans Appeals, 38 USC § 4051. See also *infra*, ch. 3 n. 1.

[2] See 28 USC § 1295 (combining two existing article III courts—the Court of Claims and the Court of Customs and Patent Appeals—into a new, article III, Court of Appeals for the Federal Circuit).

[3] For treatment of administrative tribunals in the United Kingdom, see e.g., J. A. Farmer, *Tribunals and Government* (1974); R. E. Wraith and P. G. Hutchesson, *Administrative Tribunals* (1973); Report of the Comm. on Administrative Tribunals and Enquiries, Cmnd. 218 (1957) (hereafter cited as Franks Comm. Rpt.). In New Zealand, see, e.g., Legislation Advisory Comm., Rpt. No. 3, *Administrative Tribunals* (1989) (hereafter cited as Administrative Tribunals); G. S. Orr, Report on Administrative Justice in New Zealand (printed by Gov. Printing Office) (1964) (hereafter cited as 1964 Orr Rpt.). In Australia, see Administrative Appeals Tribunal Act 1975; C. Enright, *Judicial Review of Administrative Action*, 267–81 (1985); Commonwealth Administrative Review Comm., Report, Parl. Paper No. 144 (1971) (Kerr Report), as well as the informative Annual Reports of the Administrative Review Council. In Canada, see P. Weiler, *In the Last Resort* (1974).

[4] The High Court of the United Kingdom now has several specialized units: It has a Family Division, Supreme Court Act 1981, § 5 (1)(c), a Chancery Division that contains within it a Patents Court, ibid. §§ 5 (1)(a), 6 (1)(a), and a Queens Bench Division that contains an Admiralty Court and a Commercial Court, ibid. §§ 5 (1)(b), 6 (1)(b). There are, in addition, a separate Crown Court for criminal cases, ibid. § 8, and a specialized Criminal Division of the Court of Appeal, ibid. § 3 (1). The relatively new Federal Court of Australia has jurisdiction to review almost all significant administrative agency decisions. Administrative Decisions (Judicial Review) Act 1977, §§ 5–9. And the New Zealand High Court has established a Commercial List to provide specialized treatment of commercial cases, see Judicature Act 1908, §§ 24A–24G, added by 1986 NZ Stats. No. 93, § 4, as well as the Administrative Division that is the subject of *infra* ch. 4.

[5] See, e.g., L. N. Brown and J. F. Garner, *French Administrative Law* (2nd edn., 1973); C. E. Freedeman, *The Conseil d'État in Modern France* (1961); M. J.

Nor is the first study of the specialization variable.[6] The vast majority of the existing studies however, have been confined to particular specialized courts—a tax court,[7] or an immigration court,[8] or an administrative law court,[9] or a court of international trade,[10] or a tribunal to decide disputes arising under the Freedom of Information Act.[11] And the few studies that have addressed the subject of specialized adjudication in a more general vein[12] have

Remington, 'The Tribunaux Administratifs: Protectors of the French Citizen', 51 *Tulane L. Rev* 33 (1976). See also S. G. Breyer and R. B. Stewart, *Administrative Law and Regulatory Policy*, 373 (2nd edn., 1985) (France and Italy); S. Galeotti, *The Judicial Control of Public Authorities in England and in Italy* (1954); G. S. Orr, *An Administrative Court—Its Scope and Purpose* (K. J. Scott Memorial Lecture), 5–7 (1965) (France, Italy, Belgium, Germany, and Switzerland) (hereafter cited as 1965 Orr Lecture).

[6] See nn. 7–15 *infra*.

[7] e.g. S. J. Craig, 'Federal Income Tax and the Supreme Court: The Case Against a National Court of Tax Appeals', 1983 *Utah L. Rev.* 679; E. N. Griswold, 'The Need for a Court of Tax Appeals', 57 *Harv. L. Rev.* 1153 (1944); H. T. Miller, 'A Court of Tax Appeals Revisited', 85 *Yale L.J.* 228 (1975).

[8] e.g. S. H. Legomsky, 'Forum Choices for the Review of Agency Adjudication: A Study of the Immigration Process', 71 *Iowa L. Rev.* 1297, 1386–96 (1986); P. J. Levinson, 'A Specialized Court for Immigration Hearings and Appeals', 56 *Notre Dame Lawyer* 644 (1981); M. A. Roberts, 'Proposed: A Specialized Statutory Immigration Court', 18 *San Diego L. Rev.* 1 (1980).

[9] e.g. N. L. Nathanson, 'The Administrative Court Proposal', 57 *Virginia L. Rev.* 996 (1971); G. O. Robinson, 'On Revamping the Independent Regulatory Agencies', 57 *Virginia L. Rev.* 947 (1971); 'Views of the Administrative Conference of the United States on the "Report on Selected Independent Regulatory Agencies" of the President's Advisory Council on Executive Organization', 57 *Virginia L. Rev.* 927 (1971). For a study not specific to the Ash Council Report, see L. E. Beck, 'Specialized Courts and Judicial Review of Administrative Action: An Analysis for Future Consideration' (unpublished paper, 1987).

[10] E. D. Re, 'Litigation Before the United States Court of International Trade', 26 *N.Y.L. School L. Rev.* 437 (1981); P. W. Rodino, 'The Customs Courts Act of 1980', 26 *N.Y.L. School L. Rev.* 459 (1981).

[11] 5 USC § 552. See, e.g., M. H. Grunewald, 'Freedom of Information Act Dispute Resolution', 40 *Admin. L. Rev.* 1 (1988); R. L. Saloschin, 'Proposal for an Independent Body', Remarks before the Federal Bar Assn., 8th Ann. Conf. on Openness in Government (16 Mar. 1982) (cited in Grunewald, *supra*, at 2 n. 5). The Grunewald study led to Admin. Conference of the United States, Statement no. 12 (1987), see 1987 ACUS Recs. and Reports at 1341, 1 CFR § 310.12 (1988).

[12] P. D. Carrington, D. J. Meador, and M. Rosenberg, *Justice on Appeal*, 167–84 (1976); D. P. Currie and F. I. Goodman, 'Judicial Review of Federal Administrative Action: Quest for the Optimum Forum', 75 *Colum. L. Rev.* 1, 62–85 (1975). Judge Friendly examined four potential speciality areas in H. J. Friendly, *Federal Jurisdiction: A General View*, 153–71 (patents and tax), 173–96 (administrative law and antitrust) (1973). On 19 Nov. 1988 the United States Congress established the Federal Courts Study Committee, charged with

typically been marked by two characteristics: First, rather than focus in depth on the question of specialization, they have tended to cover a whole range of forum variables—composition and independence,[13] the proper degree of geographic centralization, and an array of procedural possibilities.[14] Second, to the extent that they have isolated specialization as a separate variable, they have stopped after describing the general pros and cons of adjudication by specialists. They have not proceeded to what strikes me as the logical next question: For which groups of cases will the benefits of specialized adjudication outweigh the costs? By what criteria can such cases be identified?[15]

I believe it is crucial to isolate the specialization question and to examine it in depth. It is a question that will recur with increasing frequency as judicial backlogs conspire with heightened social and technological complexity to spur increasingly louder calls for specialized courts in widely diverse fields of law. Rather than reinvent the wheel each time a particular specialized court is proposed, it would be beneficial to have available, as a starting reference, a general set of case characteristics that favour or disfavour specialized adjudication. Once such a set has been

identifying the current problems faced by the federal courts and recommending long-range solutions. Pub. L. 100–702, Title I, 102 Stat. 4642, 4644, § 102. At the time of writing, the Committee is investigating a range of problem areas.

[13] Compositional variables include number of members, method of selecting them, their legal or other professional qualifications, and the size and qualifications of the support staff. Independence variables encompass tenure and salary protections. See generally R. H. Fallon, 'Of Legislative Courts, Administrative Agencies, and Article III', 101 *Harv. L. Rev.* 915 (1988).

[14] These would include general formality level, need for legal counsel, evidentiary rules, nature of oral and written submissions, whether decisions are made individually or collectively, speed of disposition, scope of review, standing rules, whether decisions are precedential, and whether decisions are subject to further review by another body.

[15] Currie and Goodman, *supra*, n. 12, comes closest. The authors devote section II of their article to the subject of specialized courts. Although their principal purpose is to consider the desirability of a court specializing in administrative law, they also provide some thoughtful comments on the pros and cons of specialized courts generally and discuss some possible forms that a specialist court might take. Even they, however, stop short of developing criteria for identifying those subjects for which specialized courts would be desirable. Carrington, Meador and Rosenberg, *supra*, n. 12, at 167–84, provide many thoughtful comments on the various specialization models and recommend more frequent use of internal mechanisms for assigning specified subject-matter to specified panels of judges.

assembled, the analyses of specific proposals can then concentrate mainly on ascertaining the extent to which the general characteristics are present in the particular subject-matter. I do not suggest this latter task will be mechanical; the analyst might first wish to modify the set of general factors, and in any event applying them to particular fields will require value-judgments. But at least there would exist a reasonably comprehensive, and consistent, range of considerations that could be consulted.

This book, then, will not address such questions as when adjudicators should be independent, or when they should be geographically centralized, or how formal the procedure should be, or whether adjudication should be entrusted to a 'court' rather than, or in addition to, an administrative 'tribunal'.[16] It addresses only the specialization variable, and will consider these other variables only to the extent they themselves affect the desirability of specialized adjudication. Sometimes they do. Specialization is a discrete variable, but it is not an independent variable. In some instances specialization might either advance or impede the achievement of goals usually associated with other forum attributes. Geographic dispersal, for example, might be found crucial in a given group of cases, and the total case-load might be too small to keep specialists busy in more than one location simultaneously. In that event, the preference for geographically dispersed adjudication centres might itself militate against specialization. Conversely, a conclusion that a given class of cases should be adjudicated by legal generalists would most likely result in assignment of those cases to the general courts. And taking that course would automatically settle other questions, such as whether to entrust the cases to a body with a high degree of independence, or with a relatively formal procedure. This book will note the relationships among these variables but, being concerned specifically with the question of when specialization is desirable, will leave to others the questions of when political insulation, dispersal, formal procedure, and other possible forum characteristics have independent benefit.

The first three chapters develop a general theory of specialized justice. Chapter 1 discusses the advantages and disadvantages of

[16] See text accompanying *infra*, ch. 3 nn. 1–2.

adjudication by specialists. Chapter 2 next formulates general criteria for identifying those groups of cases that would benefit from a significant degree of specialization. As the discussion in that chapter will show, these criteria apply at all stages of adjudication —initial decision-making, intermediate appeals, and final appeals, although the adjudication stage will influence the weight to be placed on certain of the criteria. Chapter 3 assumes the existence of subject-matter for which specialized adjudication is appropriate and examines the forms that such specialization might take. That chapter makes two arguments: that the evidence suggests a current trend toward *multiple*-speciality adjudicators, and that that course should be consciously pursued.

To illustrate and to test the general theory, Chapter 4 examines one such multiple-speciality model in operation: the Administrative Division of the New Zealand High Court. After summarizing its essential features, I offer my own appraisal of how particular elements of the Division have worked in practice and some suggestions for possible adjustments. This appraisal, although based in part on interviews and correspondence with the Justices and others involved in the work of the Division, represents strictly my own views.

Chapter 5 adds a final dimension: inter-nation variables that affect the suitability of specialized adjudication. That chapter examines how the case for specialization is either strengthened or weakened by such factors as a nation's system of government, legal institutions, and demography. In the process, it considers the extent to which conclusions about the effectiveness of New Zealand's Administrative Division can, despite various differences, be extrapolated to other nations.

1

The Benefits and the Costs

As the discussion in this chapter will show, entrusting adjudicative functions to specialist decision-makers can have perceptible effects on both the process and the results. Many of these effects resist clear categorization as benefits or costs. I have arranged them under three headings: the quality of the end-product, the efficiency of the process, and the acceptability of the entire package to the public.[1]

A. THE QUALITY OF THE END-PRODUCT

How does a decision to introduce specialization influence either the result of a case or, if applicable, the quality and usefulness of the reasoned opinion explaining that result? To answer that question, I have found it convenient to proceed in three steps: In what ways does specialization foster expertise? How useful is specialized expertise to an adjudicator? And how, apart from expertise, does specialization affect the quality of the product?

A specialized adjudicative unit—whether it is a court, a lower tribunal, or merely a division of either—draws its expertise from several sources. The members can be selected on the basis of their pre-existing knowledge and experience in the particular area.[2] In

[1] This grouping is a slightly modified version of the three goals that Professor Cramton has postulated for administrative processes. See R. C. Cramton, 'Administrative Procedure Reform: The Effects of S.1663 on the Conduct of Federal Rate Proceedings', 16 *Admin. L. Rev.* 108, 111–12 (1964); see also Legomsky, *supra*, Intro., n. 8, at 1313–14. I have replaced the accuracy goal with the more general goal of quality of the end-product, in order more clearly to encompass such factors as equal treatment and a well-reasoned and well-written disposition.

[2] Such selection is common for administrative tribunals. See, e.g., B. Abel-Smith and R. Stevens, *In Search of Justice*, 224–5 (1968) (UK); C. Palley, *Decision Making in the Area of Public Order by English Courts*, The Open University,

some contexts, specialization expands the selection pool by permitting the recruitment of non-lawyers whose aptitudes and specialized expertise make them suitable for membership of a specialized tribunal even though unsuitable for appointment as judges of the general courts.[3] And the creation of a specialized unit makes more feasible the hiring of a support staff composed at least partly of specialists.[4]

After appointment, expertise grows. The repetition of similar cases can solidify the members' understanding of specific sub-areas, and the diversity of cases within the specialized jurisdiction can fill the gaps in the members' knowledge of the overall scheme. If the specialized unit is part of an administrative tribunal that has both adjudicative and executive functions, then the members might also acquire familiarity with the actual implementation of the particular administrative programme.[5] Moreover, a specialized tribunal might stimulate the emergence of a specialized Bar whose members can provide the adjudicators with a continuing education. For their part, the adjudicators have a strong incentive to invest the time necessary to learn more about an area in which they will remain engaged. In particular, they have ample reason to stay abreast of developments.[6]

What good does this specialized knowledge do? Arguably it is unnecessary, at least when an adversarial procedure enables the opposing parties or their representatives to give the adjudicator

D203, block II, Pt. 3, at 43–4 (1976); J. O. Freedman, 'Expertise and the Administrative Process', 28 *Admin. L. Rev.* 363 (1976) (US).

[3] The Administrative Division of the New Zealand High Court, for example, has lay members who sit in land valuation cases, see Land Valuation Proceedings Act 1948, § 3, and in appeals from decisions of the Commerce Commission, see Commerce Act 1986, §§ 77, 78.

[4] Some scholars believe that the greatest source of expertise in administrative agencies, for example, tends to be the staff. See, e.g. 3 K. C. Davis, *Administrative Law Treatise*, § 17:1 (2nd edn., 1983); Friendly, *supra*, Intro., n. 12, at 179–80 (1973); Freedman, *supra*, n. 2, at 376.

[5] See D. R. Woodward and R. M. Levin, 'In Defense of Deference: Judicial Review of Agency Action', 31 *Admin. L. Rev.* 329, 332 (1979).

[6] The New Zealand Law Society, arguing for greater specialization within the High Court, has made the point that the inability of a generalist adjudicator to keep up to date on all areas of jurisdiction has stifled useful innovation. See First Submissions of the New Zealand Law Society to the Royal Commission on the Courts (hereafter cited as First Submission of NZ Law Society), pt. II, 1977 *NZLJ* 150, § 6.17.

all the specialized information they consider essential. The same is true when the adjudicators have access to expert staff.

The counter-argument is that those ultimately charged with making decisions best discharge the duties of their office by maximizing their own understanding and minimizing their dependence on the views of others. Moreover, advocates and staff are fallible; the use of expert adjudicators can reduce the probability of simple inadvertence. It can also reduce the chance that a party will win or lose a close case solely because of an imbalance in the quality of the advocacy. Further, the presence of more than one adjudicator in the same area of specialization and in the same physical location permits more productive collegial interchange than is possible when one's colleagues lack knowledge of the particular field.

The usefulness of specialized expertise hinges, of course, on the stage of the adjudicative process and, if the proceeding has reached the appellate stage, on the nature of the issue and the role of the adjudicator with respect to that type of issue. The strongest case for specialization can presumably be made when the adjudicator is rendering the initial decision. There is no previous decision to which to defer; the adjudicator will have to piece the case together on his or her own. As the case progresses through one or more layers of appeal, the need for specialized expertise would seem to diminish, at least if the lower tribunal has communicated its reasoning as well as its conclusion. Several judges, while conceding that some familiarity with a given area of law can be helpful to a judge performing even an appellate function, believe that the benefits of a more sophisticated expertise to one who decides appeals would be only marginal.[7]

The extent to which the value of expertise decreases from initial decision to appellate decision depends on the scope of review. And the scope of review, in turn, typically hinges on the nature of the issue. On questions of fact, at least at the initial decision-making level, expertise can aid adjudication in several ways: One who adjudicates many cases in the same field might acquire familiarity with the more frequently employed expert witnesses

[7] Interviews with Messrs Justices Chilwell (Auckland, 13 May 1988), Holland (Christchurch, 18 Apr. 1988), Greig (Wellington, 22 Apr. 1988), and Tompkins (Auckland, 13 May 1988).

and thus an enhanced accuracy in judging credibility.[8] Expertise can permit more knowledgeable assessment of technical data drawn from fields like economics, science, medicine, or engineering. Even in non-technical fields the repetition can bolster the decision-makers' understanding of the common sources of evidence in the particular subject area and the degree to which the source influences the weight that the evidence deserves. Further, if the hearing procedure permits the adjudicator to ask questions, experience in the area can enable him or her to identify lines of inquiry that the parties or their representatives have missed.

All these considerations except the last will apply with almost equal force on appeal if the appellate authority is one that has power to substitute its own judgment on questions of fact.[9] Even the last consideration—an enhanced facility to identify pertinent questions for the witnesses—will apply if the appellate authority is also empowered to take additional evidence.[10]

If the scope of review is something less than *de novo*, however, most of these considerations become less compelling. The reviewer will generally defer to the credibility assessment made by the lower tribunal,[11] which will have had the opportunity to observe the demeanour of the witness. Thus, the reviewer's lack of previous exposure to that witness will not normally be important. Similarly, even apart from expert testimony, the lower tribunal's decisions concerning the weight to be placed on the various items of evidence also typically receive great deference.[12] Still, an under-

[8] This point was made effectively by Mr Justice Jeffries of the New Zealand High Court. Interview with author (Wellington, 7 Apr. 1988).

[9] Many administrative appellate tribunals have that power. In the United States, for example, the Board of Immigration Appeals reviews *de novo* the decisions of immigration judges. See *Noverola-Bolaina* v. *INS*, 395 F.2d 131, 138 (9th Cir. 1968); *In re Vilanova-Gonzalez*, 13 I. & N. Dec. 399 (BIA, 1969). Occasionally even a court will review an agency's fact-finding *de novo*. In the United States, see, e.g., 8 USC § 1105a (a) (5) (*de novo* trial of nationality claims in deportation proceedings). In New Zealand, the Administrative Division of the High Court is empowered to rehear entirely certain categories of cases already decided by administrative tribunals. See, e.g., Land Valuation Proceedings Act 1948, §§ 26 (1), 37 (2); Accident Compensation Act 1982, § 109 (1); Sale of Liquor Act 1962, § 227 (5, 6).

[10] See the authorities cited in *supra*, n. 9.

[11] See R. J. Pierce, S. A. Shapiro, and P. R. Verkuil, *Administrative Law Process*, 358 (1985).

[12] See B. Schwartz, *Administrative Law*, 596–7 (2nd edn., 1984).

standing of an area would presumably aid the review of findings of highly technical fact, since the inferences by which one proceeds from evidence to findings might prove difficult for a non-expert. If the initial fact-finder has provided a summary of the evidence and the findings, the reviewer's need for specialized expertise will be lessened, but in a technically complex area even such a summary would not strip the reviewer's expertise of all its value.

Questions of law demand a different analysis. When adjudication of legal questions is entrusted to non-lawyers, as it sometimes is,[13] expertise in the specific field becomes a critical minimum qualification. Lawyers, in contrast, have been trained specifically to unravel difficult legal problems in unfamiliar contexts. So why would specialized expertise ever be important when legally trained adjudicators decide questions of law?[14] I suggest there are several reasons.

A benefit of expertise is its value in construing complex legislation. One approach to statutory interpretation is contextual: the adjudicator examines the document as a whole, giving special emphasis to relationships among provisions.[15] When a contextual approach is taken, expertise improves the chance that the adjudicator will be aware of provisions which were not cited by the parties but which provide insight into the meaning of the disputed clause or the reason for its inclusion. In particular, an awareness of another provision might permit the adjudicator to avoid either anomalies or loopholes. In cases where it is appropriate to consider the broad social and economic purposes of the particular statutory scheme,[16] expertise facilitates an understanding of the sometimes conflicting legislative aims.[17] If the legislative history must be

[13] In the administrative setting this can occur even at the appellate stage. See Legomsky, *supra*, Intro., n. 8, at 1308–10, 1317–20.

[14] Professor Diver, analysing the judicial role in reviewing administrative agencies' interpretations of statutes, has some useful thoughts on the benefits of the agencies' specialized knowledge in law-finding. See C. S. Diver, 'Statutory Interpretation in the Administrative State', 133 *U. Pa. L. Rev.* 549, 574–8 (1985).

[15] The European Court of Justice, for example, has been highly contextual in its interpretations of the EEC Treaty. See, e.g., L. N. Brown and F. G. Jacobs, *The Court of Justice of the European Communities*, 203–9 (1977); H. G. Schermers, *Judicial Protection in the European Communities*, 15 (2nd edn., 1979).

[16] See, e.g., E. Bodenheimer, J. B. Oakley, and J. C. Love, *An Introduction to the Anglo-American Legal System*, ch. 6 (1988).

[17] See Public and Administrative Law Reform Committee (of New Zealand), *Fifteenth Report*, para. 17 (1980) (hereafter cited as 1980 PALRC Rpt.); S. A. de

consulted to ascertain the purpose, an adjudicator with expertise in the subject area might be better able to find it.

An expert will also be more likely to recognize in other cases—either those cited by the parties or those which his or her previous knowledge itself helped uncover—similarities that would have escaped the non-cognoscenti. In this respect and in others examined below,[18] expertise can promote consistency within the specialized field. Finally, apart from the ultimate conclusion reached, expertise can improve the quality of the reasoned opinion by alerting the writer to hidden dangers, thus reducing the chance of unintentionally broad and misleading language. Conversely, knowledge of an area can enable the writer to anticipate related problems and to expose them through carefully considered dicta. For all these reasons, although expertise is less crucial when the adjudicator is reviewing a reasoned opinion around which his or her thinking might crystallize, expertise can be valuable even then.

Discretionary judgments, in which an adjudicator has the power to choose among two or more solutions,[19] are different still. I mean to include in this category of cases not only the express grant of discretion, but also the so-called 'mixed' question of law and fact,[20] where the adjudicator must apply to a set of facts a provision couched in broad, general language. It is on these questions that the usefulness of specialized expertise seems greatest. The range of the decision-maker's choice elevates the importance of understanding thoroughly the various policy considerations at work. Further, consistency would seem especially vital in matters of policy, and, as noted earlier, expertise breeds consistency within a specialized field.

Again, these considerations are somewhat weaker when the

Smith, *Judicial Review of Administrative Action*, 20 (4th edn., 1980, ed. J. Evans) (UK); H. Street, *Justice in the Welfare State*, 5–6 (2nd edn., 1975).

[18] See *infra* nn. 23–7 and accompanying text.

[19] That is a common definition of discretion. See, e.g., K. C. Davis, *Discretionary Justice—A Preliminary Inquiry*, 4 (1969); de Smith, *supra* n. 17, at 278.

[20] On the problems of classifying such mixed questions, see generally R. M. Levin, 'Identifying Questions of Law in Administrative Law', 74 *Georgetown L. Rev.* 1, 23–9 (1985); E. Mureinik, 'The Application of Rules: Law or Fact', 98 *L.Q. Rev.* 587 (1982); W. A. Wilson, 'Questions of Degree', 32 *Mod. L. Rev.* 361 (1969).

adjudicator is performing only a review function and the applicable standard of review is the familiar 'arbitrary, capricious, abuse of discretion' test.[21] When the lower tribunal has given reasons for its decision, the reviewing court need only determine whether discretion was in fact exercised, whether (after a 'hard look') all relevant considerations were taken into account and all irrelevant ones excluded, whether departures from past practice were adequately explained, and whether on balance the decision is one that a reasonable body could reach.[22] Deciding whether discretion was exercised and which factors were considered are simply matters of interpreting the challenged decision and the record accompanying it. These are not tasks that appear to call for any specialized knowledge. Assessing consistency with past practice, however, might well benefit from specialized knowledge, as discussed below. And assessing the relevance of a particular factor might require a legal determination as to whether the authority conferring the discretion—a constitution, statute, or agency regulation—was intended to permit consideration of that factor. In that case, the benefits of expertise are the same as those present in the resolution of any other legal issue and discussed above. Similarly, the relevance of a given factor can hinge on a factual judgment. When it does, the preceding analysis of the utility of expertise in fact-finding becomes equally applicable.

The remaining question is how specialization affects the quality of the end-product other than through its promotion of expertise. Improved consistency is often said to be one such benefit of specialization.[23] Within a given court or tribunal, the importance

[21] See the Administrative Procedure Act, 5 USC § 706 (2) (A).

[22] This catalogue synthesizes the common law world's leading passage on review of discretionary decisions, *Associated Provincial Picture Houses* v. *Wednesbury Corp.* [1948] 1 KB 223, 228–34 (CA) (Lord Greene, MR), with modern developments, see Amer. Bar Assn. Section of Administrative Law, 'A Restatement of Scope-of-Review Doctrine', 38 *Admin. L. Rev.* 233, 235 (1986).

[23] The inconsistency of patent law was one of the principal reasons for creating the Court of Appeals for the Federal Circuit. See S. Rep. 97–275, 97th Cong., 1st Sess., at 5–6 (18 Nov. 1981), reproduced in 1982 *US Code Cong. & Admin. News*, vol. 2, *Legis. History*, at 15–16. In New Zealand, enhanced consistency has frequently been cited as an advantage of the Administrative Division. See, e.g., Public and Administrative Law Reform Comm., First Report, *Appeals from Administrative Tribunals*, para. 32 (1968) (hereafter cited as 1968 PALRC Rpt.); Report of the Royal Commission on the Courts, para. 312 (b) (per Hon. Mr Justice

of consistency turns on the nature of the issue. Consistency would seem least important on questions of fact, since, by definition, the facts of each case turn peculiarly on the evidence. Still, given a high enough volume or a narrow enough subject, cases in which the evidence is similar are not difficult to imagine. When they do occur, concern for equality makes like findings desirable. With questions of law, however, consistency is more pressing. The same concern for equality is present, this time rooted in the principle of the rule of law, but in addition there is the element of predictability, essential to effective planning. Those seeking the favourable exercise of discretion similarly have an interest in equal treatment, although, as in the fact-finding context, their interest will surface only in those cases in which the evidence is roughly similar. When it is, they can have a strong analogous interest in predictability, since a pattern of discretionary decisions in roughly similar circumstances might well give rise to expectations and even reliance—particularly when an industry is heavily regulated and a specialized body creates many of the operative norms.

When intra-tribunal consistency is important, specialization can be beneficial. As noted earlier, specialization brings familiarity, a factor that can itself reduce the chance of inadvertent conflict. Moreover, at least if the specialized unit is set up to hear all the cases the tribunal receives within the particular speciality, consistency is improved simply because there will be fewer adjudicators whose views can potentially conflict.

Inter-tribunal conflicts present different problems. They are perhaps less important than intra-court conflicts, because the latter prevent planning even by those who know which tribunal would have jurisdiction over them. But even inter-tribunal conflicts can have negative effects. Because conflicts eventually tend to be smoothed over by higher tribunals, the temporary existence of a conflict can signal imminent change and therefore uncertainty. In addition, conflicts invite forum-shopping.[24] The problem can be minimized by establishing statutory limitations on venue, but

Beattie, Chair, 1978) (hereafter cited as 1978 Royal Comm'n. Rpt.); 1980 PALRC Rpt., *supra* n. 17, para. 17.

[24] Currie and Goodman, *supra*, Intro., n. 12, at 65.

that is not easy when a company does business in several places, and in any event there are often good reasons to authorize concurrent venue.[25]

When specialization is achieved through a system of geographically dispersed tribunals, the specialization would seem more likely to reduce intra-tribunal conflicts than to reduce inter-tribunal conflicts. The experts' deeper familiarity with the subject-matter should leave them less prone to inadvertent conflict of either type, but any adjudicators—whether generalists or specialists—might willingly reject decisions reached in other venues.

For at least two reasons, the effect of specialization on the achievement of consistency is mixed. First, depending on the form specialization takes, the trade-off can be a loss of the generalist perspective. For reasons more fully explored below,[26] the improved consistency within the speciality area might be purchased at the expense of consistency between the speciality area and other, analogous, areas. Second, even within a specialized subject area, conflicts among tribunals are not wholly bad. As others have observed,[27] the emergence of opposing views over a lengthy maturation period can aid the courts in developing their thoughts on difficult problems.

The effects described thus far tend either to favour specialization or to be mixed. Several other effects of specialization are predominantly negative. Probably the greatest—again, dependent on the form specialization takes[28]—is the loss of the generalist perspective. The value of that perspective has been emphasized by other commentators[29] and by judges.[30] Apart from its effect on

[25] See C. W. Wright, *The Law of Federal Courts*, § 42 (4th edn., 1983).

[26] See *infra*, nn. 28–30 and accompanying text.

[27] e.g. Friendly, *supra*, Intro., n. 12, at 186–7; S. Estreicher and R. L. Revesz, 'Nonacquiescence by Federal Administrative Agencies', 98 *Yale L.J.* 679, 736–7 (1989); Currie and Goodman, *supra*, Intro., n. 12, at 69–70.

[28] As to that, see *infra*, ch. 3.

[29] e.g. Carrington, Meador, and Rosenberg, *supra*, Intro., n. 12, at 168; Council on the Role of Courts, *The Role of Courts in American Society*, 139 (1984); J. S. Lubbers, 'A Unified Corps of ALJs: A Proposal to Test the Idea at the Federal Level', 65 *Judicature* 266, 274 (1981) (urging limited experiment consolidating ALJs currently assigned to certain specialized agencies); ACUS Views on Ash Council Report, *supra*, Intro., n. 9, at 931; Currie and Goodman, *supra*, Intro., n. 12, at 68–9.

[30] e.g. Interviews with Rt. Hon. Sir Robin Cooke, Pres., New Zealand Ct. of App., 12 Feb. 1988, and with Messrs Justices Jeffries, *supra*, n. 8, and Holland and

the achievement of consistency, generalized legal knowledge is important for at least two reasons. First, generalists can often find guidance or even solutions in other areas of the law. Second, generalists can be expected to approach cases with fewer preconceptions than can those who have been buried in the particular field for an appreciable time.

Specialization carries other, commonly mentioned, dangers that can be summarized briefly. The steady diet of a single type of case might deter capable individuals from either accepting appointment as members or staff personnel, or from remaining with the tribunal or court long enough for the benefits of expertise to be realized.[31] Appointment decisions are more susceptible to unhealthy lobbying influences when the appointees will be specializing in a narrow area.[32] After appointment, there arise the opposing dangers that the expert adjudicators will either develop too much sympathy for the frequently encountered specialist litigators whom they get to know or become too confident and too inclined to substitute their own views. These dangers, while cited by Professors Currie and Goodman in the context of specialized judicial review of administrative agency decisions,[33] could logically surface in any area of specialization. Again, as discussed below,[34] the specialized units can be structured so as to minimize these and other problems.

B. THE EFFICIENCY OF THE PROCESS

The efficiency of any procedure for resolving disputes has several related dimensions: the monetary costs to the public at large and to the litigants in particular; the time of the adjudicators and their

Tompkins, *supra*, n. 7; see also 1978 Royal Comm'n. Rpt., *supra*, n. 23, para. 314 (per Hon. Mr Justice Beattie) (Otago District Law Society opposed judicial specialization on basis that best judgments can be expected from judges with broad general experience).

[31] See, e.g., Carrington, Meador, and Rosenberg, *supra*, Intro., n. 12, at 168; Lubbers, *supra*, n. 29, at 274; Currie and Goodman, *supra*, Intro., n. 12, at 70; see also 1978 Royal Comm'n. Rpt., *supra*, n. 23, paras. 306, 314.

[32] See, e.g., Carrington, Meador, and Rosenberg, *supra*, Intro., n. 12, at 168; J. L. Sax, *Defending the Environment: A Strategy for Citizen Action*, 109 (1970); Currie and Goodman, *supra*, Intro., 12, at 70–1.

[33] Currie and Goodman, *supra*, Intro., n. 12, at 71–2.

[34] See *infra*, ch. 3.

support staff; and the delays at various stages from the initiation of the dispute to its ultimate resolution.[35] In all of these respects, specialization has the potential to enhance efficiency,[36] as the discussion below will show. A new specialized court can also be a device for deflecting cases from the general courts at a time when the latter are overburdened. This approach avoids the need to choose between expanding the sizes of the existing general courts and adding new general courts—both disadvantageous.[37]

The most obvious respect in which specialization promotes efficiency is that it reduces the time litigators must spend educating the adjudicators on basic aspects of the specialized area.[38] Once the fundamentals are mastered, the education process can focus on the problems specific to the case. This means less time spent by both the tribunal and the litigators, and thus a monetary saving to the public at large and to the parties. Moreover, having fewer people deciding cases within a given subject area decreases the number of instances in which two or more adjudicators will have to wrestle with the same, or a closely related, issue.

Specialization can have other procedural advantages as well. It permits the tailoring of the procedure to the subject-matter. When a tribunal must employ a common procedure for differing types of disputes, there is a risk of over-judicialization in some categories of cases[39] and too little formality in others. In the administrative context, a specialized court carries a further potential advantage:

[35] A good discussion of efficiency in the administrative process is contained in R. A. Cass, 'Agency Review of Administrative Law Judges' Decisions', in Administrative Conference of the United States, *1983 Recommendations and Reports*, 115, 155; see also Cramton, *supra*, n. 1, at 111–12 (1964).

[36] The New Zealand Law Society has cited efficiency as a general benefit of increased judicial specialization. See First Submissions of NZ Law Society, *supra*, n. 6, para. 6.13. That country's Public and Administrative Law Reform Committee cited efficiency more specifically as a benefit of the Administrative Division of the High Court. See 1968 PALRC Rpt., *supra*, n. 23, para. 33; 1980 PALRC Rpt., *supra*, n. 17, para. 17.

[37] See Currie and Goodman, *supra*, Intro., n. 12, at 25–6 n. 86; ibid. at 63.

[38] Two of the judges I interviewed specifically mentioned familiarity as a contributor to efficiency. Interviews with Messrs Justices Chilwell and Holland, *supra*, n. 7. See also Lubbers, *supra*, n. 29, at 274.

[39] Concerns about over-judicialized procedures were prominent among Professor Orr's objections to creating an Administrative Division of New Zealand's High Court. See 1965 Orr Lecture, *supra*, Intro., n. 5, at 14; 1968 PALRC Rpt., *supra*, n. 23, Minority view of G. S. Orr, para. 3 (a, d).

It can eliminate steps by replacing both the courts of general jurisdiction and one or more administrative tribunals,[40] although such an arrangement of course results in the loss of the generalist perspective as discussed earlier. Finally, as observed by Professors Currie and Goodman, channelling cases to a specialized court can avoid venue disputes as among the general courts.[41]

The effects of specialization on efficiency are not all positive. If the specialized court is assigned exclusive jurisdiction, then jurisdictional disputes between the specialized court and the general courts are always possible. On the merits, a legal generalist might be aware of an easy solution in an analogous area of law with which the specialist would have been less likely to be familiar. Further, depending on the numbers involved,[42] specialist adjudication might require long-distance travel for either the litigators or the members (and possibly staff) of the tribunal; either scenario creates additional expense. And fluctuations in volumes of case filings can produce indefinite periods in which the unit is either too busy or too idle.[43] This last problem can be serious. As at least one judge has noted, a surge of activity in one subject will often be followed by public acceptance of the case-law on that subject and then the emergence of high volumes in another, unsettled area.[44] The problem could be addressed by permitting expansion or contraction of the specialist unit at will, but that kind of arrangement is unhealthy if the members are simultaneously to possess both expertise and enough job security to attract qualified personnel and to ensure integrity in decision-making. A court of general jurisdiction is therefore better situated to absorb, over time, fluctuations in the mix of cases filed.

[40] See Legomsky, *supra*, Intro., n. 8, at 1386–7.

[41] Currie and Goodman, *supra*, Intro., n. 12, at 73–4.

[42] See *infra*, ch. 2 nn. 21–3 and accompanying text.

[43] In the United States, for example, proponents of a centralized corps of administrative law judges (in place of the present arrangement in which the ALJs are programme-specific) can be thought of as seeking to *reduce* the degree of specialization. They point to the benefit of being able to assign judges in accordance with changing volumes rather than being limited by subject-matter. See Lubbers, *supra*, n. 29, at 274 (noting argument).

[44] Interview with Mr Justice Greig, *supra*, n. 7.

C. THE ACCEPTABILITY OF THE PACKAGE

The general public's acceptance of the procedure for resolving disputes is a recognized goal of any public process.[45] A corollary is that the parties to the dispute, in particular, should be made to feel that the procedure was fair. Those points are significant because the history of specialized courts in the United States reveals mixed public reactions.[46]

Conflicting reactions are not surprising. On the one hand, a public perception of tribunal bias would seem more likely when the tribunal in question is composed of specialized experts; a person with significant experience in a particular field is likely to have formed at least tentative views on a range of issues within that field. The problem is accentuated if the adjudicator's pre-appointment position generally required advocacy of one particular side. The public might even view a specialized tribunal as qualitatively substandard—as not being a 'real' court.[47]

On the other hand, some observers believe the public will have *greater* faith in a specialized tribunal because of the deeper expertise of its members.[48] Assessments of public opinion are problematic because isolating specialization as a separate variable is difficult. One can never be certain how much of the public reaction to a given tribunal stems from the specialization feature and how much is attributable to other factors—the status of the body, the independence of its members, its ideological complexion during various periods, the cost and perceived fairness of its procedure, the adequacy of its resources, or simply the personalities of its members.

[45] See Cramton, *supra*, n. 1, at 112; accord, Cass, *supra*, n. 35, at 154–7; Currie and Goodman, *supra*, Intro., n. 12, at 4.

[46] See generally Currie and Goodman, *supra*, Intro., n. 12, at 62–3, 72–3; cf. Beck, *supra*, Intro., n. 9, at 4–53 (summarizing history of particular specialized courts in administrative law areas).

[47] See Beck, *supra*, Intro., n. 9, at 75–6; Currie and Goodman, *supra*, Intro., n. 12, at 72–3.

[48] This argument surfaced often in the debate over the Administrative Division of the New Zealand High Court. See, e.g., 1980 PALRC Rpt., *supra*, n. 17, para. 17; 1978 Royal Comm'n. Rpt., *supra*, n. 23, para. 306; 1964 Orr Rpt., *supra*, Intro., n. 3, para. 233.

2

The Criteria

A. THE GENERAL RECIPE

The preceding discussion illustrates the mixed effects of specialized adjudication. Do the benefits outweigh the costs? The answer rests on more than personal opinion; it depends also on the kind of case for which specialization is contemplated. As will be seen, certain strengths and weaknesses of specialized justice are greater in some types of cases than they are in others. This chapter offers twelve general criteria for determining whether a given class of cases should be assigned to specialist adjudicators.

A few caveats are necessary first. None of these twelve considerations is intended as either a necessary or a sufficient condition for specialization. They are, rather, merely factors that will often conflict and that will therefore require balancing. Nor do I suggest that all twelve factors are of equal stature. Judgments will be needed as to which ones command the most weight in various contexts.

Although each of these factors is relevant at all stages of the adjudication, the weight of a given factor will often hinge on the adjudication stage. Previous discussion[1] suggested the general pattern that specialization is most beneficial at the initial decision-making level and least at the appellate level. When appropriate, the discussion that follows will delineate how the application of the various specific factors will differ according to the stage the adjudication has reached.

It must be remembered too that the decision whether to employ specialist adjudicators at the initial stage and the decision whether to use them at later stages will be interdependent. In many categories of cases, there is benefit in building both specialist and generalist authority into the process at some stages. Administrative

[1] See *supra*, ch. 1 nn. 7–22 and accompanying text.

law illustrates the leading combinations. In the United States, narrowly specialized administrative agencies return decisions that are typically reviewed by administrative tribunals with equally narrow specialities, finally becoming subject to judicial review by legal generalists.[2] In New Zealand there is the same system of initial adjudication and sometimes administrative appeals—both by tribunals with narrow jurisdiction—but followed by either appeals to, or judicial review in, a High Court Division with both a general case-load and a limited specialization in most categories of administrative cases.[3] In Australia, narrowly specialized administrative bodies reach decisions that are typically appealable to a single administrative tribunal with umbrella jurisdiction over most significant categories of administrative cases and nothing else; the decisions are then ordinarily reviewable by a court whose jurisdiction similarly includes most categories of administrative cases, and very few others.[4] And in France, a separate system of administrative tribunals and courts, again with multiple-speciality jurisdiction, is in place.[5]

The comparison thus reveals a continuous spectrum from virtually no specialization in American judicial review of agency action, to some limited specialization in New Zealand, to greater (but still intermediate) specialization in Australia and France, where the jurisdiction of the reviewing courts extends to many dissimilar administrative areas rather than to a single administrative programme. Yet, while Australia, for example, employs a higher degree of judicial specialization than does the United States, the reverse is true of adjudication at the administrative level; the programme-specific American tribunals contrast with the broader, multi-programme jurisdiction of the Australian administrative appellate tribunal.

Finally, it might seem surprising at first that I do not list, as a separate factor, the magnitudes of the interests of the affected parties. The omission is deliberate. The presence of important interests is a neutral factor. It elevates the need to assure both high

[2] See, e.g., Cass, *supra*, ch. 1 n. 35; Legomsky, *supra*, Intro., n. 8, § II; Schwartz, *supra*, ch. 1 n. 12, § 7.25 and chs. 8, 9.

[3] See *infra*, ch. 4, esp. nn. 5–22 and accompanying text.

[4] See the Australian sources cited in *supra*, Intro., n. 3.

[5] See *supra*, Intro., n. 5.

quality and public acceptance, and it perhaps reduces the relative importance of expense, but those effects do not help determine whether adjudication should be entrusted to specialists. As discussed earlier, specialization can either advance or impede quality, acceptability, and efficiency, depending on other variables.

B. THE SPECIFIC INGREDIENTS

1. *Mix of Law, Fact, and Discretion*

Classifying issues as legal, factual, or discretionary is not a happy business. Categories can shade into one another, and I leave for others the precise delineation of the boundaries.[6] But the existence of borderline cases does not impair the general use of these distinctions for present purposes. For various reasons considered below, the relative frequency with which cases in a particular field present questions of law, fact, or discretion can affect the suitability of specialized adjudication. Having said that, I must concede some hesitation to include this particular factor; as the following discussion will reveal, it is debatable in which direction this factor actually cuts.

My view is that, at the initial hearing stage, a predominance of discretionary decisions *usually* favours specialization. As before, I am using the term 'discretion' to include not only decisions traditionally thought of as discretionary, but also the application of broadly worded statutory provisions or any other decisions that depend heavily on personal value-judgments. In several respects considered earlier,[7] questions to which there is a range of possible correct answers offer the greatest opportunity for the benefits of specialization to operate. The greater the scope of the decision-maker's choice, the more essential become several qualities: a deep understanding of the relevant policy objectives, a reduced probability of simple inadvertence, the pursuit of coherence, and the minimizing of dependence on the views and comparative adversarial skills of opposing counsel. All those qualities are more likely to be found in specialists who possess knowledge and experience in the specific field.

[6] For an excellent discussion, see generally Levin, *supra*, ch. 1, n. 20.
[7] See *supra*, ch. 1 nn. 19–20 and accompanying text.

My ambivalence about that conclusion stems from the recognition that, in *some* instances, the discretionary nature of the decisions is arguably a reason to *avoid* specialization. A discretionary decision, like a pronouncement of law, can make policy that affects large numbers of people in future cases. When it does, the benefits of specialization are still present but the hazards also assume greater proportion. The power to make important policy is now concentrated, perhaps dangerously, in the hands of a smaller group. Moreover, the group members are more likely than legal generalists to harbour dogmatic policy biases. Thus, although in general I regard the prevalence of discretionary questions as a factor favouring specialization at the initial hearing level, the opposite can be true when the particular types of discretionary decisions made in individual cases have ripple effects on larger groups.

The existence of a high proportion of law questions will in general weigh against specialist adjudication at the initial stages. Specialized expertise brings some advantages in the initial resolution of legal issues,[8] but legal training reduces the need for that expertise. In addition, the perspective of the legal generalist would normally be most valuable when the cases raise questions of law. Moreover, one of the benefits of specialization is that the selection pool for members can be expanded to include non-lawyer experts, a factor of least applicability to questions of law. Not all legal questions are equally amenable to generalist resolution, however; the discussion below acknowledges certain types of law questions —particularly those surfacing in technical areas—for which generalist adjudication may be less desirable.

Fact questions—especially those that have technical or other attributes favouring specialization—seem conducive to specialization at the initial decision-making stage, though less so than discretionary judgments. Consistency seems less crucial in fact-finding than in the exercise of discretion, since the latter decisions carry greater potential for the kind of policy-making that will affect future litigants. As discussed earlier,[9] however, specialists can, more easily than generalists, assess the credibility of frequently

[8] See *supra*, ch. 1 nn. 14–18 and accompanying text.
[9] See text accompanying *supra*, ch. 1 n. 8.

appearing expert witnesses and evaluate the strength of evidence secured from other familiar sources.

At later stages of adjudication, at least when the scope of appeal or review is something less than *de novo*, the preceding analysis does not apply. The typically narrow role of the reviewing tribunal on questions of fact and discretion radically diminishes the value of specialized expertise. Most such questions require the reviewing authority to do little more than examine and interpret the decision below and the accompanying record.[10] Law questions raise different kinds of considerations. On the one hand, generalist adjudicators with legal training would seem better qualified to resolve questions of law than to resolve any other category of question. On the other hand, specialization at the appellate level can promote consistent law within the particular field and permit the writing of opinions more useful to those working in that field.[11]

2. *Technical Complexity*

A high level of technicality in a particular field has traditionally been seen as an important reason to establish a specialized court or tribunal.[12] There has not always, however, been the most careful discussion of precisely what features make the subject-matter 'technical' or why those features indicate specialized adjudication.

One view might be that technical complexity can arise from the sheer size of the pertinent legislation. A massive statute, particularly if accompanied by lengthy administrative regulations, might thus be seen as introducing a high degree of 'technicality'. There is some merit to this formulation, since size alone can hinder understanding. But size should not be a concern if the subject-matter lends itself to partition into manageable, discrete parts. More important than size, therefore, is the degree of organizational complexity. When the provisions of a statutory scheme are intertwined, specialists can be particularly useful. Being familiar with the overall scheme enables them to employ a contextual approach

[10] See *Supra*, ch. 1 nn. 11–12, 21–2, and accompanying text.
[11] See *supra*, ch. 1 n. 18 and accompanying text.
[12] See, e.g. Friendly, *supra*, Intro., n. 12, at 156–8; Currie and Goodman, *supra*, Intro., n. 12, at 67–8.

to statutory construction when that course is appropriate. They will be less likely to miss developments—especially recent ones—whose bearing on the issue at hand is significant but not immediately obvious. They are likely to be most familiar with the legislative history and thus the social and economic purposes of the overall programme, a significant advantage when it is considered that relevant understandings of broad legislative purposes can often be gleaned from sources that are not specifically concerned with the statutory provision in question. Further, interrelationships among provisions create added potential for conflicts between partly related lines of cases; one who is aware of that potential can more easily head off the problem. Finally, as discussed earlier,[13] expertise improves the decision-maker's ability to draft a reasoned opinion that will avoid mistakes about the limits of the decision.

An area might also be termed 'technical' because the common sources tend to contain specialized terminology. That aspect of technicality is not as troublesome, since a legal generalist can research the meaning of those terms and can learn from the submissions of counsel. The problem lies in initially recognizing that a particular phrase *is* a specialized term whose technical meaning must be found. The presence of such terms will not always be obvious to a non-expert, particularly if a statutory term was borrowed from language in a court decision. Ideally, counsel should bring any relevant specialized terms to the attention of the adjudicator, but counsel themselves are not always specialized and even those who are might not know when the adjudicator needs help. The personal expertise of the adjudicator can therefore be beneficial.

Finally, an area might be considered technical because the *fact-finding* requires the expertise of professionals from fields other than law. Some environmental cases will be comprehensible only to chemists; some patent cases will be understood only by mechanical engineers. In those instances, even an appellate body charged only with assuring that there is evidentiary support for the findings of a lower tribunal might be mystified.[14]

In assessing the extent to which technical complexity favours

[13] See *supra*, ch. 1 nn. 15–18 and accompanying text.
[14] See Friendly, *supra*, Intro., n. 12, at 67–8.

specialization, one must consider too that there are other ways to cut through technicality. As just mentioned, counsel have an important role here. In addition, a court or tribunal might receive explanation from a specialized staff, from a specially appointed master, or, in the case of an appellate body, from the written decision under review. The effectiveness of each of these devices, however, rests on the premiss that the expert knowledge essential to the disposition of the case and to the explanation of the result can be transmitted. In some instances, that premiss might be unrealistic. Not all knowledge can be condensed into a form instantly usable by a novice. Thus, when one evaluates the weight to be assigned the technicality factor, an important consideration is the degree to which the relevant insights of the expert can be practicably transmitted to the legal generalist.

3. *Degree of Isolation*

At least two elements—discreteness and uniqueness—make some areas of law more isolated than others. I use the word 'discrete' to describe an area in which legal issues can ordinarily be resolved without reference to the resolution of legal issues in other areas. If an area is not relatively discrete—that is, if solutions to legal problems in that area will often either affect, or be affected by, solutions to other legal problems—then the benefits of consistency will generally counsel against specialization. I say generally rather than always, because it might be possible even then to create a specialized adjudicative body with jurisdiction over all such inseparable subjects. But if the related areas are individually unsuitable for specialized adjudication, or there are too many of them to permit meaningful specialization in a consolidated setting, then the only practical course might be to avoid specialization entirely.

A 'unique' area of law, as I use the term, is one in which analogies to issues outside that area are relatively infrequent. Intellectual property is a fair example. In contrast, when two or more subject areas frequently generate analytically parallel issues, there are real costs in splintering off one of them for treatment by a specialized tribunal. As mentioned earlier, the quality of a decision can be enhanced when the adjudicator is aware of approaches taken in analogous situations. That awareness can also promote consistency between or among areas. And efficiency is improved if a tribunal has ready access to a solution that avoids duplication of someone else's effort. Again, a tribunal with jurisdiction over all these analogous areas might be ideal, but when either the number or the nature of those areas makes that arrangement unworkable, specialization within one such field alone might pose unacceptable costs.

4. *Cohesiveness*

The preceding discussion suggested that a high degree of interrelationship of issues *among* several subject areas generally militates against specialization. In contrast, a high degree of interrelationship *within* a single subject favours specialization. When issues are connected, an understanding of the overall statutory scheme is of obvious benefit. Further, promoting consistency and avoiding anomaly are more difficult when resolutions of some issues have ripple effects on others; specialized expertise can reduce the problem.

5. *Degree of Repetition*

When issues that surface frequently in a given subject area are not merely related but identical, creation of a specialized adjudicative body might be worth while. The high number of similar cases elevates the importance of consistency, a goal previous discussion has shown to be furthered by specialization. The repetition also means that entrusting the decisions to a small group of specialists will promote efficiency; less initial education time will need to be invested. If repetition has a disadvantage, it might be its negative effect on the recruitment of talented members who would prefer the stimulation of diverse subject-matter.

6. *Degree of Controversy*

Subject-matter might be controversial because of the decision-makers' great latitude on questions of vital public importance. When that is the case, the previously discussed reasons for preferring legal generalists—undue concentration of power and an increased risk of bias—become operative.[15] When the source of the controversy is simply the high emotional content of the

[15] See the paragraph that follows the text accompanying *supra*, n. 7.

subject-matter, I reach the same conclusion but for additional reasons concerned with public acceptability. To the extent the public is likely to perceive bias in the decisions of specialized experts,[16] the problem is aggravated when the subject-matter stirs emotions. Further, when the volatility of the subject stems from the enormity of the individual or governmental interests at stake, then the importance of assuring acceptability is magnified, a factor that favours generalist decision-making in emotional areas.

7. *Clannishness*

In some specialized fields, the private lawyers, the government officials, the expert witnesses, and others form a relatively closed group. There might be close working relationships, and it might even be that members of some sectors of this closed group are drawn often from the ranks of other sectors of the same group. This kind of camaraderie can be quite effective. It might reduce red tape, smooth adversarial exchanges, and sustain professional associations that contribute to the creation and sharing of knowledge.

But superimposing specialist adjudicators on this type of structure is potentially unhealthy. There is always the danger that the closed nature of the group will breed complacency and stifle innovation. And when adjudicators are selected from what resembles a fraternity, the public would seem more likely to perceive, rightly or wrongly, either bias or lesser quality decisions. On balance, therefore, I regard the clannishness of a specialized community as a factor that favours adjudication by legal generalists.

8. *Peculiar Importance of Consistency*

Previous discussion noted ways in which specialized adjudication can improve consistency within the specialized field, particularly within a given court or tribunal.[17] It has been observed too that consistency is most needed on questions of law and policy.[18] Special considerations, however, can also affect the importance of consistency in a given field. If, for example, those engaged in a particular regulated activity must make long-term plans that

[16] See Currie and Goodman, *supra*, Intro., n. 12, at 71–3.
[17] See text accompanying *supra*, ch. 1 n. 23.
[18] Ibid.

require an unusual degree of certainty and predictability, then the benefits of specialization in promoting consistency become especially pronounced.

The same is true when competition within an industry magnifies the importance of equality. Unequal treatment of similarly situated individuals can always trigger resentment, but in some instances the unfairness is compounded by practical effects. If one restaurant is granted a liquor licence and an adjacent restaurant in similar circumstances is denied one, the latter is worse off than if both licence applications had been denied. The good fortune of one business can, in a competitive setting, be the bad fortune of another. In contrast, a decision to grant one person's application for social security disability benefits would not ordinarily compound the harm to another similarly situated person whose application had been denied—apart, again, from the creation of resentment. The presence of these or other special circumstances that make consistency within a given field peculiarly important favour specialized adjudication.

9. *Dynamism*

A rapidly changing subject-matter would seem on balance to favour specialization. To the extent that a narrowly defined jurisdiction and the attendant risk of monotony might ordinarily hamper the recruitment of capable adjudicators, the dynamic nature of the field might make the work more stimulating and thus lower the recruiting barriers. Moreover, the increased need to monitor and apply current developments makes specialized expertise more valuable. If the changeability of the law is built-in—if, for example, the specialized area is a single programme that is intended from the start to be only temporary—then an additional reason to assign the adjudicative function to a specialized tribunal is that the tribunal can be disbanded when the programme ends.

The changeability of the law does not, however, point unambigously in one direction. Changes can reduce the volume of litigation—as, for example, in a climate of deregulation[19]—thus

[19] Mr Justice Chilwell of the New Zealand High Court predicted, for example, that the number of liquor licensing cases will drop dramatically if the government implements its recent proposals to ease substantive restrictions on the sale of alcohol. Interview with Mr Justice Chilwell, *supra*, ch. 1 n. 7.

leaving a specialized tribunal permanently overstaffed. But the changeability of the law can as easily increase the volume of litigation. New provisions might require new determinations in individual cases or create uncertainty about the meaning of existing rules. In addition, even when the changes are expected to reduce the volume, the problem might be addressed, admittedly at some cost,[20] by building flexibility into the terms of office or by adopting the kind of multi-speciality arrangement recommended in Chapter 3 below. All things considered, therefore, a high degree of changeability is a factor that favours specialized adjudication.

10 *Logistics: Volume, Time per Case, and Geographic Distribution*

The volume of litigation in a given subject area is highly relevant to the wisdom of establishing a specialized adjudicative body. When a system of courts of general jurisdiction is strained by the size of its case-load, and all reasonable efforts have already been made to reduce the total number of cases requiring final adjudication,[21] then three basic options will remain: adding new general courts, expanding the sizes of the existing general courts, and transferring selected groups of cases to specialized courts. The first two options are problematic for reasons discussed elsewhere.[22] When there is independent reason to single out a class of cases for specialized adjudication, high volume can therefore reinforce the benefits of doing so. That is particularly true if the cases, in addition to being numerous, are individually time-consuming.

[20] If the tenure rules leave the adjudicators too vulnerable to dismissal, the resulting arrangement could impair independence, the appearance of justice, and effective recruiting. See Legomsky, *supra*, Intro., n. 8, at 1396. And adoption of the multiple-speciality model, even though positively viewed in *infra*, ch. 3, does have disadvantages discussed in that chapter.

[21] e.g. various forms of alternative dispute resolution.

[22] Professors Currie and Goodman, see *supra*, Intro., n. 12, point out that adding new federal circuits can lessen geographic diversity within a circuit, increase inter-circuit conflicts, and aggravate the problem of undue influence by individual Senators in the appointment process, though they do not seem to regard any of those disadvantages as both serious and insurmountable. Ibid. at 25–6 n. 86. They observe that the alternative strategy of adding new judgeships to the existing circuits can impair collegiality, an element to which they attach great importance. Ibid. at 63.

Just as a high volume of cases can impair the functioning of the general courts, a low volume can make specialized adjudication ineffectual. So much of the *raison d'être* for specialized tribunals is the enhanced expertise, consistency, and efficiency that specialization can bring. All these benefits require a sufficient case-load.

A low volume will be exceptionally lethal to the operation of a specialized adjudication system if there is also a need for geographic dispersal. A small pie is inconvenient enough, but having to carve it into even smaller segments exacerbates the problem. If, for example, it is thought necessary that adjudication of a class of cases be available on a regular basis in several major population centres, and the total volume of such cases is small, then either the specialized adjudicators will be frequently idle or their jurisdiction will have to be so significantly broadened that they can no longer be portrayed accurately as specialists.[23] The problem can of course be attacked by authorizing adjudicators to ride circuit, but that approach too entails monetary costs.

11. *Special Need for Prompt Resolution*

For several reasons, specialized adjudication can be a device to speed the disposition of cases. Experts can presumably handle greater case-loads because their familiarity with the subject diminishes the time they will need per case. Further, if the authority creating a specialized tribunal wishes, it can tailor the resources of the tribunal to the special need for promptness in that subject area—an option not as readily available when the cases comprise merely one small part of the work of a tribunal with general jurisdiction. In addition, conflicts within a given subject area can slow the ultimate resolution of legal issues; therefore, to the extent that specialization reduces conflict, it also furthers promptness.

In some contexts, the disposition time is especially crucial because there exists an incentive to file frivolous actions for purposes of delay.[24] To the extent specialization increases speed,

[23] As discussed in chs. 4 and 5 *infra*, that is the present problem in New Zealand.

[24] The Immigration and Naturalization Service, for example, believes that large numbers of deportation appeals are filed solely as delaying tactics, although it is not at all clear that the INS claims are not exaggerated. See Legomsky, *supra*,

it reduces the time bought by a delaying tactic, thus dampening the incentive to file. If the result is to measurably discourage frivolous actions, then the reduced case-load should make the process speedier still. Further, if an adjudicative body chooses to attack the delay problem by establishing a procedure for screening out frivolous cases at an early stage, a specialist can more safely and more confidently identify those cases in which the arguments are frivolous.

12. *Unique Procedural Needs*

No one procedure is ideal for all disputes. An advantage of a specialized adjudicative unit is that its procedures can be tailored to the attributes of its cases. A given group of cases might best be handled by a relatively informal procedure that the general courts would be ill-equipped to employ.[25] If the area is one generally marked by a low quality of advocacy, the procedural rules could be structured to give the adjudicator an active role in the development of the evidence. And, even if it is decided to use the same procedural rules as those applied in formal courts of general jurisdiction, the expertise of the adjudicator reduces his or her dependence on the effectiveness of counsel and blunts the effects of an imbalance in the skills of opposing counsel. In these and other ways, the need for procedural devices peculiar to a given area will be a factor that favours specialized review.

Intro., n. 8, at 1335–7. Similar perceptions of delay can surface in any context in which a person retains the benefits of the status quo while proceedings are pending.

[25] This is one of the most commonly cited reasons for the spread of administrative tribunals. See, e.g., de Smith, *supra*, ch. 1 n. 17, at 20; Franks Comm. Rpt., *supra*, Intro., n. 3, §§ 38, 406; H. W. R. Wade, *Administrative Law*, 777, 779 (5th edn., 1982); Wraith and Hutchesson, *supra*, Intro., n. 3, at 259.

3

The Models

Suppose the criteria discussed in the preceding chapter point toward specialized adjudication for a given group of cases. What form should that specialization take? This chapter examines the components of the possible models and argues for greater use of multiple-speciality adjudication systems.

A. THE VARIABLES

In theory, there are as many possible models of specialized adjudication as there are combinations of forum variables. In practice, certain combinations are unknown or unrealistic or both. I have found it convenient to separate the variables into two groups: those relevant to all adjudicative bodies and those relevant only to specialized units.

Most adjudicative bodies are commonly described as either 'courts' or administrative 'tribunals', but the distinction seems more an intuitive one based on tradition and status than an analytical one defined by functional or structural attributes.[1] Further, even a body easily classifiable as court or tribunal might be subdivided into smaller organizational units whose attributes render them functionally equivalent to separate adjudicative entities. Since these distinctions are difficult to draw, and since in any event the discussion that follows will not rest on them, they will be discarded here in favour of the more general term 'adjudicative unit'. I use this phrase, therefore, to describe any court, tribunal,

[1] Many writers, noting the difficulties of distinguishing courts from tribunals, have treated them as differing only in degree. See, e.g., Abel-Smith and Stevens, *supra*, ch. 1 n. 2, at 224–8; P. P. Craig, *Administrative Law*, 170 (1983); Farmer, *supra*, Intro., n. 3, at 184–9; S. H. Legomsky, *Immigration and the Judiciary—Law and Politics in Britain and America*, 282–3 (1987); Palley, *supra*, ch. 1 n. 2, at 43–4.

or division of court or tribunal whose work consists of adjudicating individual cases.[2]

Apart from names, adjudicative units vary in a number of ways: How much control do other governmental officials have over those who do the adjudicating? How many members are there? How high is their pay? How are they appointed, and by whom? How is their tenure defined? What qualifications must they possess? In particular, must they be lawyers? Over what subject-matter does the unit have jurisdiction? Is that jurisdiction exclusive? Is it original or appellate? If it is appellate, what is the scope of review? Is the decision itself reviewable by another body? How formal is the procedure? Is it adversarial or inquisitorial, with or without juries, with our without legal counsel? How formal are the rules of evidence? Are decisions made individually or collegially? Are the decisions precedential? Are they published? Is the body a single centralized unit, or is it geographically dispersed?

Other variables that belong in that list can surely be identified. I am more concerned here, however, with a second cluster of variables: those who applicability is confined to *specialized* adjudicative units. These latter variables have one element in common. All are concerned with the degree of specialization—that is, with the location of the unit on the continuous spectrum from generalism to narrowly defined specialization. Again there are several recognized models in practice. They differ in three respects.

One variable is the breadth of the specialized jurisdiction. The subject-matter might be confined to a single field, or a number of specialized fields might be consolidated in a single unit. Further, a single field of specialization might itself take up either a narrow area or a broad area. At one extreme is the administrative agency that has jurisdiction over a single, esoteric programme. Other administrative agencies and even courts[3] possess jurisdiction over single programmes that cut wider swaths.

As the following discussion will show, however, there is today a movement toward more frequent use of arrangements that combine two or more unrelated or only vaguely related subjects in a

[2] As for those bodies whose functions include both adjudicative and other responsibilities, my analysis is intended to apply only to the former.

[3] See, e.g., the courts cited in *supra*, Intro., n. 1.

single specialized adjudicative unit. Examples of actual and proposed multiple-speciality structures abound.[4] In the United States, the recently established Court of Appeals for the Federal Circuit has appellate jurisdiction over most cases involving patents, international trade, non-tort claims against the federal government, Merit Systems Review Board decisions, Court of Veterans Appeals decisions, and a few miscellaneous others.[5] The simultaneously created Claims Court has trial jurisdiction over all non-tort claims against the federal government, an area that encompasses, among others, contract cases and tax refund cases.[6] The Court of Appeals for the DC Circuit has exclusive jurisdiction to review certain specified federal administrative agency decisions.[7] The Temporary Emergency Court of Appeals has jurisdiction to decide a number of specific issues.[8] For several years, controversial proposals to consolidate the administrative law judges now employed by individual government agencies into a single centralized corps have been the subject of serious debate. The differing forms of the proposed consolidations would give rise to further examples of multi-speciality arrangements.[9]

Elsewhere, the Family Division of the High Court of the United Kingdom has been assigned certain matrimonial cases, certain cases concerning the status of children, and certain probate

[4] In addition to the examples in which the judges themselves are specialized, there is the analogous structure of the central legal staff of the Court of Appeals for the Ninth Circuit. The members have been grouped into three multiple-speciality divisions that together occupy all areas of federal appellate jurisdiction. Telephone Conversation with Professor Dinah Shelton, Director, Central Legal Staff, US Court of Appeals for the Ninth Circuit (29 Aug. 1988).

[5] See Beck, *supra*, Intro., n. 9, at 21–6. See also 38 USC § 4092 (exclusive jurisdiction to review decisions of Court of Veterans Appeals).

[6] Beck, *supra*, Intro., n. 9, at 26–9.

[7] Ibid. at 52–3; Currie and Goodman, *supra*, Intro., n. 12, at 75. In practice, the Court of Appeals for the DC Circuit has achieved a high degree of specialization in other areas of administrative law as well. In 1986, it received almost 30% of the nation's appeals from administrative agencies; in that year, 73% of its case filings were appeals from agencies or from district court decisions involving the government. P. M. Wald, Speech to Amer. Bar Assn. Section of Admin. Law, Washington, DC, 9 Oct. 1987, reproduced in 40 *Admin. L. Rev.* 508, at 508–9 (1988).

[8] Beck, *supra*, Intro., n. 9, at 44–8.

[9] One proposal would establish a unified ALJ corps composed of several divisions, each comprising several related specialities. See V. W. Palmer and E. S. Bernstein, 'Establishing Federal Administrative Law Judges as an Independent Corps: The Heflin Bill', 6 *Western New England L. Rev.* 673, 680, n. 39 (1984). A proposal for a limited experiment consolidating some of the existing ALJs is

cases.[10] In New Zealand, several modern proposals for multi-speciality arrangements have been considered: Professor Gordon Orr once proposed an Administrative Court that would have sat in several divisions, each responsible for designated subject areas.[11] The Royal Commission on the Courts, several years later, stopped short of recommending the establishment of additional specialized High Court divisions, but did urge greater use of informal mechanisms for assigning judges case types with which they had acquired familiarity.[12] And the Legislation Advisory Committee, appointed by the Minister of Justice, recently proposed replacing the individual administrative appellate tribunals with a few larger ones, each responsible for several subject areas.[13]

My own view is that the increasingly common arrangements in which all or most categories of administrative law cases have been funnelled into a single adjudicative unit represent a broader example of the multiple-speciality operation. Such a characterization requires only that administrative law be viewed for present purposes as a collection of diverse administrative programmes rather than as a single, unified, subject area.[14] Without trivializing

another form of multiple specialization. See Lubbers, *supra*, ch. 1 n. 29; see also J. S. Lubbers, 'Federal Agency Adjudications: Trying to See the Forest and the Trees', 31 *Fed. Bar News & J.* 383 (Nov. 1984) (repeating call for pilot programme).

[10] Supreme Court Act 1981, sched. 1, para. 3.

[11] See 1964 Orr Rpt., *supra*, Intro., n. 3, §§ 236–44; 1965 Orr Lecture, *supra*, Intro., n. 5, at 16; 1968 PALRC Rpt., *supra*, ch. 1 n. 23, Minority view of G. S. Orr, para. 4. Although Professor Orr's proposal was not adopted, it was instrumental in stimulating governmental consideration of some form of judicial specialization in administrative law. Ultimately Parliament established the Administrative Division of the High Court, discussed in *infra*, ch. 4.

[12] See 1978 Royal Comm'n. Rpt., *supra*, ch. 1 n. 23, para. 317; ibid. at 97 (Rec. No. 6).

[13] Administrative Tribunals, *supra*, Intro., n. 3, paras. 118–40.

[14] Whether that characterization is more generally correct is of course a matter of great controversy. The American administrative law case-books reflect the divergent views of the editors as to whether the subject-matter is best organized by general principles of administrative law or by specific administrative programmes. Compare, e.g., G. O. Robinson, E. Gellhorn, and H. H. Bruff, *The Administrative Process* (3rd edn., 1986) with W. Gellhorn, C. Byse, P. L. Strauss, T. Rakoff, and R. A. Schotland, *Administrative Law Cases and Comments* (8th edn., 1987). For a middle ground, see Breyer and Stewart, *supra*, Intro., n. 5 (generally organized by common principles,with exceptional coverage of several specific agencies).

the important general principles that unite the law of judicial review of administrative agency decisions, I would none the less maintain that, for purposes of assessing the benefits and costs of specialized expertise, it is the size and complexity of particular statutory schemes—not the mastery of judicial review principles—that are most relevant. Broadcast regulation cases, immigration cases, environmental cases, and tax cases, it seems to me, have more substantive law differences than administrative law similarities, at least for purposes of those comparisons that bear on the desirability of specialized adjudication.

If that depiction is accepted, then still further evidence of the trend toward multiple-speciality adjudicative units is plentiful. The Administrative Courts that form integral parts of the legal systems of France and several other European nations have long been in operation,[15] but other developments are more modern. New Zealand's Administrative Division, examined at length in the next section, is one such example. Australia's Administrative Appeals Tribunal, noted earlier,[16] is another. So, too, is the Federal Court of Australia, the jurisdiction of which extends to most major categories of administrative cases.[17] And at least one Australian state—Victoria—has established its own general administrative appeals tribunal.[18]

A second variable that influences the degree of specialization is the extent, if any, to which those who have specialized jurisdiction also hear general cases. At one end of the spectrum is the administrative tribunal, which has *only* specialized jurisdiction. In the United States, the Claims Court and the Court of Appeals for the Federal Circuit, though possessing fairly wide specialized jurisdiction, are staffed by judges who similarly have no grant of general jurisdiction.[19]

In contrast are those arrangements in which the judges who exercise a specialized jurisdiction do so only part-time, spending most of their time on their general case-loads. One such structure is that in which one United States regional court of appeals is given exclusive jurisdiction over specific subject-matter. The Court

[15] See *supra*, Intro., n. 5.

[16] See *supra*, Intro., n. 3.

[17] See *supra*, Intro., n. 4.

[18] See Administrative Tribunals, *supra*, Intro., n. 3, para. 103.

[19] See *supra*, nn. 5–6 and accompanying text.

of Appeals for the DC Circuit, for example, has jurisdiction over certain environmental and other miscellaneous cases.[20] Another approach is to create a specialized court whose members are simultaneously judges on courts of general jurisdiction. The leading United States example is the Temporary Emergency Court of Appeals, the members of which are district and circuit judges occupied principally with their general judicial work.[21] New Zealand's Administrative Division is another form that fits this category; its members spend the vast bulk of their time on general High Court cases.[22] And the recommendations of the New Zealand Law Society for informally assigning cases based on the special experiences of particular judges[23] would also have entailed adjudication by generalist judges with some limited measure of specialized responsibility.

A third variable effecting the degree of specialization is the duration of the adjudicators' responsibility over the specialized subject-matter. Specialized expertise is maximized when the adjudicator serves in a specialized capacity permanently or at least indefinitely—that is, when there is no built-in expiry date for the specialized term. It is possible, however, to make use of temporary specialists. An adjudicator might be appointed to a specialized unit for a fixed term with no expectation of renewal. This unit might be a separate entity, as was true, for example, of the now defunct Commerce Court in the United States,[24] or a specialized division of a more general adjudicative body might be staffed on a rotating basis by permanent members of that body.

B. THE ARGUMENT FOR THE MULTIPLE-SPECIALITY UNIT

I have previously resisted narrowly specialized adjudication, at least at the judicial level.[25] But multiple-speciality adjudication is different, and in this section I urge greater use of it, particularly

[20] See Beck, *supra*, Intro., n. 9, at 52–3; Carrington, Meador, and Rosenburg, *supra*, Intro., n. 12, at 172; Currie and Goodman, *supra*, Intro., n. 12, at 75. See also *supra*, n. 7 (Court of Appeals for DC Circuit in practice becoming specialist in several administrative programmes).

[21] See Beck, *supra*, Intro., n. 9, at 44–8.

[22] See *infra*, ch. 4.

[23] First Submissions of NZ Law Society, *supra*, ch. 1 n. 6, §§ 6.19–6.21.

[24] See Currie and Goodman, *supra*, Intro., n. 12, at 71–2.

[25] Legomsky, *supra*, Intro., n. 8, at 1386–96.

within larger courts. As the discussion below will illustrate, the middle ground that a multiple-speciality approach occupies between legal generalism and narrow specialization gives it great future potential. While some of that potential exists at the initial decision-making stage, it is greatest at the appellate stage.

Decreasing the degree of specialization naturally deflates both the benefits and the costs of specialized adjudication. As discussed earlier, there are in turn three major ways to soften the degree of specialization: by combining specialities, by making the specialized work only a part of the case-loads of the affected adjudicators, and by providing for only temporary service of those adjudicators in a given specialized unit. Thus, the multiple-speciality approach is just one of several devices to alter the balance of costs and benefits in specialized adjudication. Not surprisingly, therefore, the logic of most of the comments below will not be confined to the multiple-speciality strategy; it will be seen to extend to the whole notion of intermediate specialization. None the less my argument here focuses on the multiple-speciality model, and at the close of this section I explain why I emphasize that strategy over the other hybrid models.

A final qualification is that I assume, throughout this discussion, that in a multiple-speciality unit *all* the members of the unit have multiple specialities. One could devise a multi-member unit in which each member takes on a different, narrowly defined, speciality. But the benefits and costs of that course would be the same as one in which each member is conceived as a one-person, single-speciality, unit. Thus, if the pros and cons of single-speciality and multiple-speciality arrangements are to be usefully compared, the latter must be defined in a way that makes each individual member a specialist in more than one area.

With those introductory comments, it is possible to examine the effects of multiple specialization. I begin by conceding a negative effect: a lower level of expertise than is possible with a single-speciality model. The expertise is less for several reasons. While a single-speciality unit can be staffed by those with existing experience in the particular area, one is not likely to find suitable individuals whose experience happens to lie in precisely the combination of areas over which a multiple-speciality unit has jurisdiction. Thus, the latter starts off with less expertise. Further, since the time of the multiple-speciality adjudicators will be divided among several subjects, expertise will not grow as rapidly as it will when the members can work steadily on a single subject.

Still, while multiplying the number of specialities makes the attainment of real expertise less likely, it should not prevent the development of basic familiarity, provided the number and complexity of the combined specialities are kept within reasonable bounds. At least at the appellate stage, the incremental value of expertise becomes marginal once the threshold level of familiarity has been achieved, for reasons considered earlier.[26] Moreover, even in a multiple-speciality unit, there is an incentive to stay reasonably up to date. There is, as well, the opportunity for collegial interchange with other members conversant with the subject-matter.

More important, this marginal sacrifice of specific expertise permits the purchase of substantially all the benefits of legal generalism. The members are exposed to a diverse case-load. The benefits of a generalist perspective lie principally in the value of analogy; the multiple-speciality model would seem at least as likely as the general jurisdiction model to expose the adjudicators to analogous cases. It might even be argued that, if anything, the multiple-speciality approach is more likely to sprout productive analogies because the specialities that are combined can be deliberately selected with an eye toward that goal.

Inadvertent conflict within a given subject area might be more likely in a multiple-speciality unit than in a single-speciality one. But the difference in likelihood would again seem marginal, since the members' basic familiarity with the subject-matter should ordinarily assure at least the identification of potential conflicts. Once a problem is identified, the members are in a position to choose between reconciliation and repudiation. In that effort they have not only their own general knowledge and special familiarity, but also, possibly, access to expert counsel and expert staff. Further, being familiar with other related areas, they are in a better position than the single-speciality expert, and arguably in at least as good a position as the generalist adjudicator, to promote consistency between related areas.

The multiple-speciality model also averts or diminishes the

[26] See *supra*, ch. 1 nn. 7–22 and accompanying text.

other, previously discussed,[27] quality-related dangers of specialized adjudication. Introducing an interesting mix of subjects reduces the monotony that might otherwise hamper the recruitment of talented individuals. The dangers of heavy lobbying in the appointment process are similarly lessened. Since the members' exposure to specific areas will be more dispersed, there is not the same likelihood as in a single-speciality unit of developing improper sympathy for a single agency or another frequent litigant. For the same reason, the members are appreciably less likely to become over-confident and unduly assertive in substituting their own policy views for those of legislators or other government officials. Finally, the combination of more adjudicators and less intensively involved adjudicators tempers the biases sometimes associated with single-speciality bodies. In all these ways, the multiple-speciality unit can, in appropriate settings, optimize the quality of the end-product by combining the positive attributes of specialists and generalists.

A multiple-speciality approach can also promote efficient use of scarce adjudicative resources. Basic familiarity reduces education time,[28] though admittedly not as dramatically as would the degree of expertise that flows from devotion to a single speciality. Proper selection of the consolidated specialities permits the tailoring of the procedure to the needs of the particular subject areas. Broadening the jurisdiction to cover several specialities makes it more feasible to locate the units in smaller population centres, thus reducing the amount of necessary travel. And combining specialities can be an efficient way to absorb fluctuations in the volume of cases filed in a single specialized subject area.[29]

Finally, the combination of specialities might well ease problems of public acceptability by reducing perceptions of either bias or substandard adjudicators. At the same time, the members' basic familiarity with the subject-matter should instil a higher degree of confidence than might be experienced with generalists.

For all these reasons, therefore, I suggest that the multiple-speciality model should be used more frequently, at least at the

[27] See *supra*, ch. 1 nn. 31–4 and accompanying text.

[28] At least two of the judges whom I interviewed cited increased efficiency as a benefit of familiarity with the subject-matter. Interviews with Messrs Justices Chilwell and Tompkins, *supra*, ch. 1 n. 7. Accord, Letter from the Chief Justice to the author, 12 May 1988, para. 1.

[29] Administrative Tribunals, *supra*, Intro., n. 3, para. 106 (5).

appellate stage. I recognize, however, that the benefits I have described could be largely achieved by adjusting, instead, the other determinants of degree of specialization: the proportion of members' time spent on non-specialized jurisdiction and the duration of the members' specialized assignment. The strategy is intermediate specialization, not merely the multiple-speciality device for achieving it.

None the less, I have deliberately emphasized the multiple-speciality feature over these other instruments of intermediate specialization. What distinguishes a unit whose jurisdiction consists entirely of several designated specialities from one whose work combines one narrow speciality with a general case-load is what the members are doing with their time when they are not working on cases in a particular assigned area. In the former model, the members are working on some other specialized area. In the latter model, they are working on general cases. Because I assume the existence of many different subjects that would benefit from some degree of specialization, I prefer the multiple-speciality arrangement as a means of bringing the benefits of specialization to a greater number of areas for which specialization is thought suitable. Further, as noted earlier, the benefits associated with generalism seem at least as prevalent in the multiple-speciality model as they are in a model that combines a single speciality with a general jurisdiction.

A system of rotating the members in and out of specialized units does have real benefits—most notably the reduction of staleness and bias and perhaps greater attractiveness in recruiting. The trade-off, of course, is the loss of the knowledge that a specialist accumulates in the course of the job, including the incentive to invest appreciable time in learning more about the specialized area.

In any event, these three vehicles for achieving intermediate specialization are not mutually exclusive. A unit could, for example, be assigned several specialities *and* a general case-load.[30] Further, no matter how the specialized jurisdiction is defined, the appointments of the adjudicators could be made either permanent or temporary.

[30] e.g. the Administrative Division of the New Zealand High Court, discussed *infra*, ch. 4.

4

The Multiple-Speciality Model in Operation: New Zealand's Administrative Division

Whether in political affairs[1] or in legal matters, New Zealand has been known for innovation. It was the first country to grant the vote to women.[2] It was the first English-speaking country to establish an Ombudsman's office.[3] The New Zealand accident compensation scheme, which replaces several important areas of tort law, is legendary.[4] With much less fanfare New Zealand also charted, in 1968, what was then a radical course in administrative law. It established a special division of its High Court to hear appeals from the decisions of those administrative tribunals that Parliament would later designate.[5] This chapter examines the background and operation of the Administrative Division and assesses its effectiveness in promoting the objectives for which it was created.

Like the United States, New Zealand has established a variety of forums in which individual disputes are resolved. It has a large number of administrative tribunals and other specialized

[1] New Zealand's non-nuclear policy is the most notable modern example.

[2] See Electoral Act 1893, §§ 3 ('"person" includes woman'), 6; Rpt. of the Royal Commission on the Electoral System, *Towards a Better Democracy*, App. A, § 4.3 (1986).

[3] G. Palmer, *Unbridled Power—An Interpretation of New Zealand's Constitution and Government*, 204 (2nd edn., 1987).

[4] For a summary, see Accident Compensation Corp., *The New Zealand Accident Compensation System* (1984). For some thoughtful comments on the application of the New Zealand accident compensation scheme to medical injury cases, see W. Gellhorn, 'Medical Malpractice Litigation (U.S.)—Medical Mishap Compensation (N.Z.)', 73 *Cornell L. Rev.* 170, 188–202 ([1988).

[5] Judicature Amendment Act 1968.

adjudicative bodies that assert jurisdiction in narrowly defined areas.[6] There are, in addition, a number of bodies that in practical terms can be regarded as courts of general jurisdiction. The geographically scattered district courts (formerly called magistrates' courts) are given civil jurisdiction under several specific headings that together make up quite a broad range of cases, ordinarily subject to a monetary limit of NZ$12,000.[7] The district courts also conduct preliminary hearings in the most serious criminal cases, and have trial jurisdiction in other criminal cases, including, sometimes, jury trials.[8]

The High Court (formerly called the Supreme Court) is New Zealand's superior court of general jurisdiction. It hears both civil cases and criminal cases, and it has both trial jurisdiction and jurisdiction over appeals from the district courts.[9] Its thirty-two judges[10] sit regularly in various cities throughout New Zealand.

The Court of Appeal hears appeals from the High Court, the district courts in certain cases, and certain administrative tribunals.[11] It consists of the Chief Justice (ex officio), the President of the Court of Appeal, and five other High Court Justices,[12] all appointed permanently to the Court of Appeal. It ordinarily sits in Wellington, in panels of three.[13]

[6] See the lists provided in Administrative Tribunals, *supra*, Intro., n. 3, Apps. I, II; Palmer, *supra*, n. 3, at 93. As in the United States, there are also 'courts of special jurisdiction' not analytically distinguishable from the administrative tribunals. See Law Comm. Rpt. No. 7, *The Structure of the Courts*, App. B at 214–15 (1989) (hereafter, The Structure of the Courts).

[7] See The Structure of the Courts, *supra*, n. 6, at 215–16. There are 98 district court judgeships, see District Courts Act 1947, § 5 (2), some of which are on the Family Court or the Children and Young Persons Court (both part of the district courts), or on various administrative tribunals. The Structure of the Courts, *supra*, at 215–16. At present there is no Administrative Division of the district courts; the possibility of creating one has been raised, Administrative Tribunals, *supra*, Intro., n. 3, paras. 105–6, but rejected in favour of a proposal to group the existing tribunals into three larger bodies, ibid., paras. 118–40. See generally 'The District Courts—An Interview with Sir Desmond Sullivan, Chief District Court Judge', 1985 NZLJ 88.

[8] See The Structure of the Courts, *supra*, n. 6, App. B, at 219–20.

[9] Ibid. at 222–6.

[10] The Judicature Act 1908, § 4 (1), authorizes the appointments of a Chief Justice and 31 other High Court Justices. Those figures, however, include the six Court of Appeal judges. Ibid. § 57 (2)(c).

[11] For a good description, see The Structure of the Courts, *supra*, n. 6, at 226–8. It also has some very limited original jurisdiction. Ibid. at 226.

[12] Judicature Act 1908, § 57 (2)(c).

[13] The Structure of the Courts, *supra*, n. 6, at 226.

4. *A Multiple-Speciality Model in Operation*

The Judicial Committee of the Privy Council, sitting in London, at least for the moment hears both appeals as of right and discretionary appeals from the New Zealand Court of Appeal, as well as occasional appeals from the High Court.[14] In October 1987, however, the government announced its intention to abolish Privy Council appeals.[15] In a thorough 1989 report proposing a range of reforms, the Law Commission recommended that, upon abolition of Privy Council appeals, the present Court of Appeal be replaced with a 'Supreme Court' that would then become the final court of New Zealand.[16]

A. BACKGROUND

The earliest significant impetus for an adjudicative unit specializing in administrative law was the 1964 Report of then Crown Counsel Gordon Orr.[17] At the time of that Report, there existed in New Zealand a vast number of administrative tribunals. The methods of obtaining redress from their decisions were diverse and complex. To describe the differing remedies, it is first necessary to explain the distinction drawn in New Zealand between appeal and review.

In New Zealand,[18] as in the United Kingdom,[19] statutes often authorize 'appeals'—sometimes to courts, sometimes to other bodies—from the decisions of specified administrative agencies. These appeals vary enormously in the latitude they afford the appellate body to set aside the decision. Some statutory appeals permit full, *de novo* reconsideration of all issues; other statutes authorize appeals 'as if from the exercise of discretion'; still other appeals are on point of law only; and some are limited to fairness grounds.[20]

Even in the absence of a statutory appeal right, however, the New Zealand High Court ordinarily has inherent, common law,

[14] Ibid. at 228–9.

[15] Ibid., para. 615.

[16] Ibid. at xiii, Rec. No. 7.

[17] 1964 Orr Rpt., *supra*, Intro., n. 3.

[18] See ibid., paras. 283–9.

[19] See de Smith, *supra*, ch. 1 n. 17, at 19–20, 126, 402; P. J. Dalton and R. S. Dexter, *Constitutional Law*, 202–3 (1976); see also Tribunals and Inquiries Act 1971, § 13 (1) (UK).

[20] Administrative Tribunals, *supra*, Intro., 3, para. 37 (f).

supervisory jurisdiction to 'review' the decision of an administrative body. The review function traditionally has been conceived as limiting the court to searching for an error that goes to jurisdiction, an error of law on the face of the record, or an error that concerns procedural fairness.[21] So characterized, the court's review powers are generally envisioned as being narrower than the powers asserted on appeal. For at least two reasons, that depiction is misleading today. First, as noted above, 'appeals' in New Zealand can themselves take various forms, some of them quite narrow. Second, whatever the theoretical limitations on the scope of review, Sir Kenneth Keith has demonstrated that in practice the judicial powers actually asserted on appeal sometimes do not exceed those asserted on review (though at other times they are much wider).[22]

The Orr Report illustrated the variety of appellate and review mechanisms then in place. The Supreme Court (as it was then called) had general supervisory jurisdiction to *review* the decisions of statutory administrative bodies that performed judicial functions.[23] In doing so, however, it was encumbered by complex technical limitations on the available remedies—the prerogative writs of certiorari, prohibition, and mandamus, and, to an increasing extent, declaratory and injunctive relief.[24] In contrast, most administrative decisions were not subject to *appeal* at all.[25] Those that were appealable went to different places. The appellate

[21] See 1964 Orr Rpt., *supra*, Intro., n. 3, paras. 283–9; *Amin* v. *Entry Clearance Officer* [1983] 2 All ER 864, 868 (HL) (per Lord Fraser of Tullybelton); *Chief Constable of the North Wales Police Force* v. *Evans* [1982] 1 WLR 1155, 1174 (HL) (per Lord Brightman).

[22] K. J. Keith, 'Appeals from Administrative Tribunals—The Existing Judicial Experience', 5 *Victoria U. of Wellington L. Rev.* 123 (1969); see also R. Cooke, 'The Struggle for Simplicity in Administrative Law', in M. Taggart (ed.), *Judicial Review of Administrative Action in the 1980s*, 1–17 (1986); R. Davison, 'The Role of the Courts in Modern Society', 4 *Otago L. Rev.* 277, 281 (1979). In the United Kingdom, the expansion of the scope of judicial review has been traceable largely to two factors: (*a*) the growing tendency to label errors as jurisdictional and (*b*) the increased frequency with which the statutes and rules governing administrative tribunals require them to provide reasons, a factor that makes it more likely any legal errors will appear on the face of the record. See S. H. Legomsky, *Immigration and the Judiciary—Law and Politics in Britain and America*, 14–15 (1987).

[23] 1964 Orr Rpt., *supra*, Intro., n. 3, paras. 284–9.

[24] Ibid., paras. 284, 292.

[25] Ibid., para, 221; accord. R. Wild, 'The Administrative Division of the Supreme Court of New Zealand', 22 *U. of Toronto L.J.*, 258, at 258 (1972).

authority was sometimes a magistrates' court (as it was then called), sometimes a statutory administrative tribunal, and sometimes the applicable Minister.[26] Occasionally, though not often, appeal lay to the Supreme Court.[27]

The Orr Report made a number of sweeping recommendations. Many of them, not directly pertinent to the present discussion, concerned tribunal procedure.[28] One of Professor Orr's proposals (since adopted) was to simplify judicial review by replacing the prerogative writs with a single form of review in which the grounds for setting aside the administrative decision would be a uniform, slightly expanded, version of the then existing grounds.[29] Most important here, the Orr report recommended the creation of an Administrative Court that would hear appeals from most significant administrative decisions.[30]

The proposed Administrative Court would have taken over the appellate jurisdiction of the various bodies discussed above and would have heard appeals from other administrative bodies whose decisions previously had not been appealable at all.[31] The status of the court was to lie between those of magistrates' courts and the Supreme Court.[32] Each judge was to be assigned to a particular division; each division would have handled cases that fall within a particular subject-matter grouping.[33] The Court would have had not only appellate jurisdiction, but also review jurisdiction.[34] The decisions of the Administrative Court would themselves have been appealable to the Court of Appeal.[35]

[26] See 1964 Orr Rpt., *supra*, Intro., n. 3, paras, 223, 226–7, and 283, respectively.

[27] Ibid., paras. 224–5.

[28] The Report recommended, for example, the enactment of an American-style Administrative Procedure Act setting down procedural guidelines that would balance the benefits of flexibility and uniformity. Ibid., paras. 215–18. It also urged safeguards concerning the appointment and tenure of tribunal members. Ibid., paras. 187–91.

[29] See ibid., paras. 292–301. Parliament moved a step in that direction in 1972 when it established a simplified procedure known as the application for review. See Judicature Amendment Act 1972, § 4, as amended by Judicature Amendment Act 1977, § 13.

[30] 1964 Orr Rpt., *supra*, Intro., n. 3, ch. 13.

[31] Ibid., para. 229.

[32] Ibid., para. 235.

[33] Professor Orr tentatively suggested divisions for licensing, local planning, land valuation, industrial cases, state services, taxes, and trade practices, in addition to a general division for certain miscellaneous cases. Ibid., paras. 236–44.

[34] Ibid., paras. 245–6.

[35] Ibid., paras. 258–9.

Professor Orr saw many advantages in that structure. He felt it would enhance the uniform implementation of administrative justice; permit decision by judges more interested than the then existing Supreme Court Justices were in administrative law; allow the pooling of experience in analogous areas; furnish a greater incentive to create a body of settled principles; and bolster public confidence in the administrative system.[36]

The Orr report was controversial. Two other non-governmental reports soon appeared; they both preferred to channel appeals to the Supreme Court rather than to create a new Administrative Court.[37] The Minister of Justice appointed a Public and Administrative Law Reform Committee (PALRC), composed of distinguished authorities conversant with administrative justice, to investigate the whole subject of administrative tribunals. Their first report, published in 1968, focused on the problems of appeals.[38] Pertinent excerpts are reproduced in the appendix to the present book.

A majority of the Committee believed strongly that the decisions of administrative tribunals should generally be appealable to the ordinary courts. The Committee regarded legal qualifications as essential to the performance of the appellate function.[39] It cited the Law Society's conclusions that, in the eyes of the community, 'justice administered by bodies other than the ordinary courts tends, from the point of view of fairness and care, to be an inferior brand of justice', and that such a perception was not 'wholly without foundation'.[40] At the same time, the Committee perceived disadvantages in assigning appeals from specialized administrative bodies to the ordinary courts. Its principal concern was that judges had generally been uninterested in the then emerging field of administrative law, and, consequently, too ready to defer to the expertise and policy responsibilities of the administrative bodies.[41]

[36] 1964 Orr Rpt., *supra*, Intro., n. 3, ch. 13, paras. 228–34.

[37] See the reports of the New Zealand section of the International Commission of Jurists and the New Zealand Law Society, summarized in Wild, *supra*, n. 25, at 260–1.

[38] 1968 PALRC Rpt., *supra*, ch. 1 n. 23. The committee's charge is described in para. 1. See also J. F. Northey, 'An Administrative Division of the New Zealand Supreme Court—A Proposal for Law Reform', 7 *Alberta L. Rev.* 62, at 62–3 (1969).

[39] 1968 PALRC Rpt., *supra*, ch. 1 n. 23, para. 9.

[40] Ibid., para. 19.

[41] Ibid., para. 11.

Its recommended solution was to create, within the Supreme Court, a special division that would hear appeals from designated administrative bodies.[42] This approach, the Committee felt, would promote expertise, consistency, economy of effort, and the public perception of a fair and thorough process—all without sacrificing the benefits of an administrative tribunal system.[43]

Several features of the Committee's proposed Administrative Division are noteworthy: The Division would have jurisdiction over both appellate and review cases.[44] Its members, to be chosen by the Governor-General, would do general Supreme Court work as well as Administrative Division work.[45] Appointees would ideally possess, in addition to the usual Supreme Court Justice qualifications, 'a full appreciation of the need to give effect to the economic and social policies the legislation was designed to implement'.[46] Lay members were to be eligible to sit with Supreme Court Justices in appropriate cases.[47] The expense and formality levels of the proceedings hopefully would not exceed those of the proceedings conducted by the existing appellate administrative tribunals.[48] In cases where it is found appropriate to permit an appeal on a point of law from the decision of the Administrative Division, the appeal would go to the Court of Appeal.[49]

In recommending the Administrative Division, the PALRC majority rejected the Administrative Court proposal of Professor Orr. It reached several conclusions: A separate Administrative Court would inherently be of lower status than the Supreme Court, thus impeding public acceptance and hampering recruitment of members.[50] If the new Court were given the same status as the Supreme Court, the decisions of the two courts might conflict.[51] Finally, the Committee thought it important that the supervisory jurisdiction to review the decisions of administrative

[42] Ibid., paras. 31, 35. The Committee proceeded to identify several specific tribunals whose decisions should be appealable to the Administrative Division. Ibid., paras. 43–87.

[43] Ibid., paras. 12, 31, 33, 35, 37.

[44] The Division 'would also exercise the present jurisdiction of the Supreme Court in administrative law'. Ibid., para. 35.

[45] Ibid., para. 36 (i).

[46] Ibid., para. 36 (ii).

[47] Ibid., para. 36 (iii).

[48] Ibid., para. 36 (iv, v).

[49] Ibid., para. 40.

[50] Ibid., para. 34 (i).

[51] Ibid., para. 34 (iii).

bodies remain with the Supreme Court, and that appellate and review jurisdiction not be separated.[52]

Professor Orr, himself a member of the Committee, dissented. He feared over-judicialized procedure; a tendency of Supreme Court Justices to shy away from the kinds of controversies often raised in appeals from administrative decisions; a loss of the impartiality essential to the functioning of the Supreme Court; a loss of informality and jurisdictional flexibility; and, inevitably, a lesser likelihood of specialization and consistency than would be possible with an Administrative Court.[53] He found the majority's objections to an Administrative Court unpersuasive. Professor Orr did not accept that a unified court whose jurisdiction embraced as broad and important a field as administrative justice would be perceived as lower in stature than the Supreme Court; in any case, he suggested, that concern could be accommodated by making each member a Supreme Court Judge.[54] As for the fear that a separate Administrative Court would breed conflicts with the Supreme Court, he observed that any such conflicts could be resolved by permitting appeal to the Court of Appeal on points of law.[55]

Within a few months of publication, most of the recommendations of the PALRC majority were enacted into law. The Judicature Amendment Act 1968 established an Administrative Division of the Supreme Court, leaving for future statutes the job of filling in its jurisdiction with specific grants.[56] The Act also authorized the issuance of administrative Rules concerned with practice, procedure, and costs.[57] Such Rules were issued the following year and replaced with a new set in 1985.[58]

[52] 1968 PALRC Rpt., *supra*, ch. 1 n. 23, para. 34 (iv).

[53] Ibid., App. para. 3.

[54] Ibid., App. para. 5.

[55] Ibid., App. para. 6. Professor Orr pointed out also that the potential for conflict would be no greater with an Administrative Court than with an Administrative Division. Ibid. See also, J. A. Farmer, 'Administrative Division of the Supreme Court—An Experiment in Administrative Suicide', 1969 NZLJ 106 (sharing Professor Orr's concerns about over-judicialization).

[56] The Act amended the Judicature Act 1908 by repealing sections 25 and 26 and adding new sections 25, 26, 26A, and 26B. See Judicature Amendment Act 1968, § 2.

[57] Judicature Act 1908, § 26B.

[58] See High Court Rules, pt. IX, §§ 676–700 (1985) (hereafter cited as Administrative Division Rules), replacing Supreme Court (Administrative Division)

B. ON PAPER AND IN PRACTICE

1. *Jurisdiction*

The list of statutes that authorize appeals to the Administrative Division has grown steadily over the years. Today, the vast majority of those significant administrative decisions that are appealable to the High Court have been assigned to the Administrative Division.[59] These appeals range from questions of law only,[60] to questions of law and selected questions of fact,[61] to full rehearing of all issues.[62] There exists no current complete list of all the statutes that confer jurisdiction on the Administrative Division,[63] but Table 1 sets out all the provisions I have been able to find.

If there are patterns in the selection of administrative decisions for appeal to the Administrative Division, I am unable to distil them. The selected decisions represent a wide range with respect to such variables as the nature of the individual interest (for example property, liberty, etc.), the magnitudes of the individual and governmental interests, the procedure and composition of the tribunal whose decision is being appealed, the types of issues (legal, factual, discretionary), and the degrees of technicality, complexity, and controversy. A previous writer concluded, as I do, that the legislative grants of Administrative Division

Rules 1969. The new Rules are reproduced as sched. I to Judicature Amendment Act (No. 2) 1985, amending Judicature Act 1908, sched. II.

[59] See Administrative Tribunals, *supra*, Intro., n. 3, App. 3.

[60] e.g. Town and Country Planning Act 1977, § 162 (1). In practice, however, the term 'law' is of course capable of broad construction. See J. F. Northey, 'A Decade of Change in Administrative Law', 6 *N.Z.U.L. Rev.* 25, 33 (1974).

[61] e.g. Sale of Liquor Act 1962, §§ 226, 227, 229 (fact questions concerning character of liquor licence applicant are appealable).

[62] e.g. Land Valuation Proceedings Act 1948, § 26 (1).

[63] No such list is maintained by the Department of Justice, the Registrar's Office, or the office of the Chief Justice. The list that appears in W. J. Sim and G. Cain, *The Practice of the High Court and Court of Appeal of New Zealand*, 14 (1987), omits quite a number of applicable statutes. See Table 1. The Legislation Advisory Committee, however, has now compiled a list of the major statutory grants of Administrative Division jurisdiction, with principal concentration on those administrative programmes that are discussed elsewhere in its report. See Administrative Tribunals, *supra*, Intro., n. 3, App. 3.

TABLE 1. *Statutes Conferring Jurisdiction on Administrative Division*

Accident Compensation Act 1982, § 111
Air Services Licensing Act 1983, § 33
Animal Remedies Act 1967, § 34
Beer Act 1977, § 10
Broadcasting Act 1976, §§ 61, 84
Chiropractors Act 1982, § 35
Citizenship Act 1977, § 19
Clean Air Act 1972, § 35
Coal Mines Act 1977, § 79
Commerce Act 1986, §§ 75, 91
Contraception, Sterilization and Abortion Act 1977, §§ 26, 28
Co-operative Dairy Companies Act 1978, §§ 18A, 19
Customs Acts Amendment Act (No. 2) 1976, §§ 28, 29
Dieticians Amendment Act 1979, § 12
Distillation Act 1971, §§ 11, 20
Electrical Registration Act 1979, § 44
Films Act 1983, § 37
Fisheries Act 1983, § 49
Fishing Industry Board Act 1963, § 35A
Gaming and Lotteries Act 1977, § 65
Gas Act 1982, §§ 27, 28
Human Rights Commission Act 1977, §§ 42, 63
Immigration Act 1987, §§ 115, 117
Land Act 1948, § 133
Land Valuation Proceedings Act 1948, § 2
Land Valuation Proceedings Amendment Act 1968, § 2 (extending Administrative Division jurisdiction to several related statutory schemes)
Local Government Act 1974, § 37A
Massage Parlours Act 1978, § 33
Medical Practitioners Act 1968, § 2
Milk Act 1967, § 57G
Mining Act 1971, § 239
Motor Vehicle Dealers Act 1975, § 130
Nurses Act 1977, § 49
Passports Act 1980, § 9
Pesticides Act 1979, § 70
Pharmacy Act 1970, § 40
Plant Varieties Act 1973, § 30
Private Investigators and Security Guards Act 1974, § 64

Real Estate Agents Act 1976, § 112
Sale of Liquor Act 1962, § 230A
Social Security Act 1964, § 12Q
Soil Conservation and Rivers Control Act 1941, § 103
Superannuation Schemes Act 1976, § 19
Tobacco Growing Industry Act 1974, § 38
Toxic Substances Act 1979, § 67
Town and Country Planning Act 1977, § 162
War Pensions Act 1954, § 85A

---

jurisdiction over the years 'generally reflect an "ad-hoc" approach'.[64]

The PALRC Report had recommended that the Administrative Division be granted not only appellate jurisdiction in specified areas, but also the then existing general supervisory jurisdiction of the Supreme Court to review administrative adjudication.[65] At the urging of the Judiciary,[66] however, Parliament chose instead to give the Chief Justice the discretion to refer such applications to the Division.[67] After criticism of that arrangement,[68] the Chief Justice in 1975 issued a Practice Note declaring that those applications 'which involve matters dealt with by tribunals in respect of whose decisions there is a right of appeal to the Administrative Division will be referred to the Division'.[69] The Note went on to say that other applications for review would be heard under the Court's general jurisdiction.[70] Although future commentary continued to urge that all applications for review of administrative decisions ordinarily be channelled to the Administrative Division,[71] the law has not been changed.

64 D. P. Ryan, 'A Review of the Administrative Division of the High Court', 109 (LL M Thesis, Victoria University of Wellington, Faculty of Law, 1980).

65 1968 PALRC Rpt., *supra*, ch. 1 n. 23, para. 35 ('the present jurisdiction of the Supreme Court in administrative law'). See also Northey, *supra*, n. 60, at 28; J. F. Northey, 'The Administrative Division of the New Zealand Supreme Court: A Postscript', 15 *Alberta L. Rev.* 186, 187 (1977).

66 See Northey, *supra*, n. 65, at 187.

67 Judicature Act 1908, § 26 (c).

68 e.g. Northey, *supra*, n. 60, at 42.

69 Practice Note [1975] 2 NZLR 345.

70 Ibid.

71 'New Zealand Law Society Recs. to the Royal Comm'n. on the Courts', (hereafter cited as NZ Law Society Recs.), 52 *Lawtalk* 2, para. 21 (1977); 1978 Royal Comm'n. Rpt., *supra*, ch. 1 n. 23, para. 312 (c); Northey, *supra*, n. 65, at 187.

Conversely, Parliament invested the Chief Justice with the discretion to divert to a non-Administrative Division judge an appropriate case over which the Administrative Division would otherwise have jurisdiction.[72] Analogous criticisms have been voiced.[73]

Finally, the appellate decisions of the Administrative Division are not themselves appealable to the Court of Appeal unless the particular statutory scheme expressly so provides.[74] In practice, however, the major statutory sources of Administrative Division jurisdiction now expressly provide some form of further appeal to the Court of Appeal.[75]

At least as important as the authorized jurisdiction of the Administrative Division, are the actual quantity and distribution of its cases. To learn more about the actual operation of the Administrative Division, I compiled statistics concerning the activities of the Division from its inception until the end of 1987. I had available two particularly useful sources: an elaborate numerical chart prepared as part of an LL M thesis by Mr D. P. Ryan, covering cases decided until the end of 1979;[76] and a log, maintained by the Registry of the New Zealand High Court, in which certain details of each Administrative Division case are entered.[77]

[72] Judicature Act 1908 § 26 (3). This power has been exercised very infrequently. See *infra*, nn. 82–3 and accompanying text.

[73] Ryan, observing that PALRC had recommended the creation of this power so that a judge with special qualifications could be assigned in a given instance, suggested that the Chief Justice had in fact used the power for temporal or geographic convenience. See Ryan, *supra*, n. 64, at 22. Others have argued that the power should be invoked only when an Administrative Division judge is not reasonably available. See 1978 Royal Comm'n. Rpt., *supra*, ch. 1 n. 23, paras. 310, 312(b); N.Z. Law Society Recs., *supra*, n. 71, para. 21.

[74] Section 66 of the Judicature Act 1908, which generally authorizes the granting of leave to appeal from the High Court to the Court of Appeal, is inapplicable to Administrative Division decisions other than applications for review, unless another statute expressly provides otherwise. Ibid. § 26 (4).

[75] e.g. Land Valuation Proceedings Act 1948, §§ 18, 18A; Town and Country Planning Act 1962, § 162H; Accident Compensation Act 1982, § 112 (1); Motor Vehicle Dealers Act 1975, § 131; Passports Act 1980, § 10; Contraception, Sterilization, and Abortion Act 1977, § 27.

[76] See Ryan, *supra*, n. 64, App. IV. Another useful Table, covering the period 1969–76, appears in Northey, *supra*, n. 65, at 188.

[77] This particularly helpful log is maintained by the Deputy Registrar, Mr David Mangos.

4. *A Multiple-Speciality Model in Operation*

The statistical summaries that follow[78] must be read with several qualifications in mind: All tables refer to cases finally decided, not to cases filed or heard. I have excluded cases that were settled before final judgment, cases that were abandoned, and log entries that were simply dispositions of motions for extensions of time, motions for rehearing, or other procedural motions the inclusion of which would have resulted in double-counting. Occasionally, the Registry's log omitted important information or described the subject-matter jurisdiction in terms that were too cursory for present purposes. In most such instances, I was able to glean complete information from individual case files. In some instances, however, the case files had been sent to other High Court registries throughout the country. In those few latter situations, the Deputy Registrar was ordinarily able to fill in the gaps by personal recollection. Finally, except where specified otherwise, I have counted both appeals and applications for review. The latter, which are few in number,[79] are included under the category 'Other', regardless of subject-matter.

Table 2 presents an overall picture of Administrative Division activity from its inception until the end of 1987. As it illustrates, the Administrative Division decided 556 cases in its first nineteen years—an average of 29 per year. Its jurisdiction has been dominated by a few areas. The land cases—valuation (typically for property tax or eminent domain purposes) and planning—alone account for almost half the cases. Together with the next four most frequent categories, they comprise 78 per cent of all cases decided by the Administrative Division to date.[80]

Applications for review have not been a large part of the Division's diet. In its first nineteen years, the Division decided only 43 applications for review,[81] an average of two per year. The low numbers can probably be ascribed to the widening appellate jurisdiction that, when applicable, permits the aggrieved party to

[78] I have retained my original worksheets and would be glad to furnish copies upon request. These worksheets contain data extracted from the Administrative Division log noted in text accompanying *supra*, n. 77.

[79] See *infra*, n. 81 and accompanying text.

[80] The absolute figures are 432 out of 556.

[81] Of these, 33 were decided between 1969 and 1979. See Ryan, *supra*, n. 64, App. IV, Table 6. Eleven were decided in one year, 1978. Ibid. During the period 1980–7, ten more were decided. See worksheets, *supra*, n. 78.

TABLE 2. *Aggregate Disposition of Cases by Subject Matter*[a] *(1 January 1969 to 31 December 1987)*

Valuation of Land	135
Town and Country Planning	131
Liquor Licensing	79
Accident Compensation	39
Sales Tax Assessments*	26
Broadcasting Licences[b]	22
Fisheries*	12
Motor Vehicle Dealers Licences*	12
Commerce Commission	8
Immigration*	7
Real Estate Agents Licences	5
Other (including 43 applications for review)	80
Total	556

* The asterisked items are ones that were not broken down separately in Ryan's 1969–79 summaries. Thus, the figures appearing above for these items include only the 1980–7 decisions. Since the specific categories separated out in Ryan's summaries accounted for all but 8 cases decided over the 11-year period he studied, the omission is insignificant.

[a] Each figure in this table is the sum of the applicable figures for 1969–79, and 1980–7. The former were extracted from Ryan, *supra*, n. 64, App. IV, Table 7 (Totals Column). The latter are from my own worksheets, *supra*, n. 78.

[b] Although Ryan's Table 7, *supra*, n. 64, shows a total of 15 Broadcasting Act cases, the actual number is 14 for reasons he notes at the conclusion of his table. Combined with the 8 cases from 1980–7, the total figure is therefore 22.

avoid the limitations attending applications for review. There is unfortunately no practicable way to discover how many applications for review are decided outside the Administrative Division, since the High Court records do not segregate those administrative law cases that are not assigned to the Division. For the same reason, it is not feasible to count the precise number of instances in which the Chief Justice has exercised his statutory power to

Table 3. *Decisions of the Administrative Division by Year and Subject Matter*[a]

	Land Valuation	Planning	Liquor Licensing	Accident Compensation	Sales Tax[b]	Broad-casting	Other	Total
1969	19	0	4	0	—	2	2	27
1970	21	0	7	0	—	0	4	32
1971	7	3	5	0	—	2	2	19
1972	10	8	3	0	—	5	0	26
1973	4	6	4	0	—	0	3	17
1974	7	8	2	0	—	0	3	20
1975	8	6	0	0	—	0	2	16
1976	18	8	1	0	—	0	8	35
1977	10	6	5	3	—	2	4	30
1978	8	8	12	4	—	2	8	42
1979	5	5	8	6	—	1	8	33
1980	2	4	4	11	0	1	13	35
1981	3	10	1	1	2	0	15	32
1982	1	15	6	3	2	3	7	37
1983	1	10	7	2	13	0	10	43
1984	6	14	3	3	6	0	15	47
1985	3	5	4	3	0	1	9	25
1986	2	7	1	1	2	1	5	19
1987	0	8	2	2	1	2	6	21
Total	135	131	79	39	26	22	124	556

[a] As in Table 2, the numbers shown for each individual subject category include only appeals; applications for review are included in the column labelled 'Other'. For years 1969–79, the numbers are the sums of the figures appearing in Ryan, *supra*, n. 64, App. IV, Tables 5 and 6. For 1980–7, the figures are extracted from my worksheets, *supra*, n. 78.

[b] Precise volumes for 1969–79 unknown but negligible. See Table 2.

divert from the Administrative Division a case that is within its jurisdiction.[82] Chief Justice Davison assured me, however, that that power is 'sparingly and rarely exercised'.[83]

The figures in Table 2 provide a rough overview of the Administrative Division's work. Viewed in isolation, however, they conceal radical changes in the work of the Division during the period. Whether because new substantive law generates new issues, or because a flurry of published court decisions in a given area reduces the need for future litigation in that same area, the mix of Administrative Division cases has varied dramatically over the years. Table 3 illustrates the changes.

2. *Personnel*

The Administrative Division consists of seven High Court Justices.[84] In practice, one of the members has always been the then Chief Justice.[85] In certain case categories described below, lay members may also sit.[86] Each High Court judge has a staff of one—an associate, not legally trained, who performs administrative functions; no judge has a personal law clerk.[87] Although the PALRC Report had recommended selection of members by the Governor-General,[88] Parliament decided to vest the appointment power in the Chief Justice,[89] a controversial issue discussed below.[90]

The PALRC Report had also hoped that, whoever makes the appointments, the members chosen would have not only the qualities generally required of a High Court Justice, but also an

[82] See Judicature Act 1908, § 26 (3).

[83] Chief Justice letter, *supra*, ch. 3 n. 28, at 3. The Chief Justice added that the power is used only when a hearing is urgent and no Administrative Division judge is available.

[84] Judicature Act 1908, § 25 (2).

[85] See Table 4. At the time of the present study, Chief Justices Wild and Davison had been the only two Chief Justices since the creation of the Administrative Division. On 6 Feb. 1989, Chief Justice Davison retired and was replaced as Chief Justice and Administrative Division member by the Rt. Hon. Sir Thomas Eichelbaum.

[86] See *infra*, nn. 100–9, and accompanying text.

[87] Chief Justice letter, *supra*, ch. 3 n. 28, para 6 (g). There are a few law clerks not assigned to particular judges.

[88] 1968 PALRC Rpt., *supra*, ch. 1 n. 23, para. 36 (i).

[89] Judicature Act 1908, § 25 (2). See, e.g. Northey, *supra*, n. 60, at 28.

[90] See *infra*, § C. 4.

appreciation of the need to further the social and economic purposes of the particular legislation.[91] Whether that criterion has actually figured in the appointment decisions is not clear. Chief Justice Davison, questioned about the factors affecting his selections, would say only that he chose those judges who had 'a particular ability in the administrative field'.[92] Others have identified a range of likely factors, including length of judicial experience,[93] pre-judicial experience in administrative law,[94] and location.[95] For their part, most of the High Court Justices whom I interviewed believed that the judges were generally indifferent about serving on the Administrative Division,[96] although one suggested that experienced judges would feel slighted if not offered the opportunity.[97] Chief Justice Davison, in contrast, perceived the Administrative Division as a popular assignment.[98]

Once appointed to the Administrative Division, judges have remained there until they have either left the bench or gone to the Court of Appeal.[99] As a result, service on the Division tends to last several years. Table 4 summarizes the service of the nineteen Administrative Division members from the inception of the Division to 31 December 1987.

The Act that created the Administrative Division contemplated the appointment of voting lay members eligible to sit with High Court Justices in particular categories of cases, but left the designation of those categories for future statutes.[100] The two principal case types for which specialized lay-members have now been authorized are land valuation cases and Commerce Commission cases.[101] In each of these settings, the lay members are appointed by the Governor-General—two members serving five-year terms

91 1968 PALRC Rpt., *supra*, ch. 1 n. 23, para. 36 (ii).

92 Chief Justice letter, *supra*, ch. 3 n. 28, para. 6 (a).

93 e.g. Interview with Mr Justice Holland, *supra*, ch. 1 n. 7; Telephone Conversation with the Deputy Registrar, David Mangos, 10 June 1988.

94 Interview with Mr Justice Tompkins, *supra*, ch. 1 n. 7.

95 Interview with Professor G. S. Orr, 16 Feb. 1988.

96 Interviews with Messrs Justices Jeffries, Holland, and Greig, *supra*, ch. 1 nn. 7, 8.

97 Interview with Mr Justice Holland, *supra*, ch. 1 n. 7.

98 Chief Justice letter, *supra*, ch. 3 n. 28, paras. 6 (a), 6 (b).

99 Telephone Conversation with Mr Mangos, *supra*, n. 93.

100 Judicature Act 1908, § 26A.

101 Land Valuation Proceedings Act 1948, § 3 (1, 2); Commerce Act 1986, §§ 77,78. See also Human Rights Commission Act 1977, § 66.

TABLE 4. *Service on the Administrative Division*[a]

	Approx. yrs. of service	Yr. appointed to Division	Yr. left Division
Speight, J.	13	1969	1982
Davison, CJ[b]	10+	1978	—
Wild, CJ	10	1968	1978
White, J.	9	1973	1982
Chilwell, J.[b]	6+	1982	—
Jeffries, J.[b]	6+	1982	—
Woodhouse, J.	6	1968	1974
Bisson, J.	6	1981	1987
Wilson, J.	4	1969	1973
McMullin, J.	4	1976	1980
Roper, J.	4	1981	1985
Casey, J.	4	1982	1986
Holland, J.[b]	3+	1985	—
Tompkins, J.[b]	2+	1986	—
Greig, J.[b]	2+	1986	—
Mahon, J.	2	1980	1982
Doogue, J.[b]	1+	1987	—
McGregor, J.	1	1968	1969
Cooke, J.	0	1976	1976

[a] The years in which the judges joined and left the Administrative Division were supplied by Chief Justice Davison. See Chief Justice letter, *supra*, ch. 3 n. 28, Attachment. Since the exact dates were not furnished, I have estimated the length of service by subtracting the year the judge was appointed from the year he left. In each case, therefore, the actual service could vary from the estimate by as much as one year. The average error should thus be about six months.

[b] Current member of Administrative Division. Years of service estimated by subtracting appointment year from 1988.

in the case of land valuation and an unspecified number serving terms of up to five years in the case of commerce.[102] The Land Valuation Proceedings Act does not specify the qualifications of the lay members. The Commerce Act expressly requires 'knowledge or experience in industry, commerce, economics, law, or

[102] Land Valuation Proceedings Act 1948, § 3 (1, 2); Commerce Act 1986, § 77 (1, 3). Each of these sections also permits reappointment. The Human Rights Commission Act 1977, § 66 (1), authorizes the judges themselves to appoint two additional members to hear particular cases.

accountancy'.[103] Under each statute a quorum consists of a High Court judge and at least one lay member,[104] except that a High Court judge may sit alone in certain instances, including unopposed orders, cases in which the parties agree to dispense with lay members, cases in which the only issues are 'substantially' questions of law, and applications for leave to appeal to the Court of Appeal.[105] A decision of the court requires the vote of the High Court judge *and* at least half the total panel.[106] If the High Court judge is outvoted by lay members, the case is referred to the Court of Appeal for decision.[107]

In actual practice, fourteen of the eighteen land valuation cases decided from 1 January 1980 to 31 December 1987 have been heard by a High Court judge sitting with a lay member.[108] Of the five Commerce Commission cases decided during this period, lay members were used in only one.[109]

The statistics reveal some extremely interesting patterns in the distribution of Administrative Division cases to the various members. The patterns concern both the quantity and the nature of the case assignments. Table 5 illustrates the quantities but it must be read with caution. It says nothing about the various judges' general, non-Administrative Division, case-loads. It does not purport, therefore, to gauge the overall productivity of individual judges. In addition, even with respect to the intensity of the judges' Administrative Division case-loads, the figures are

[103] Commerce Act 1986, § 77 (2).

[104] Land Valuation Proceedings Act 1948, § 13 (1); Commerce Act 1986, § 77 (9). Accord, Human Rights Commission Act 1977, § 66 (2).

[105] Land Valuation Proceedings Act 1948, § 13 (4); Commerce Act 1986, § 77 (14).

[106] Land Valuation Proceedings Act 1948, § 13 (2); Commerce Act 1986, § 77 (10, 11); accord, Human Rights Commission Act 1977, § 66 (4).

[107] Land Valuation Proceedings Act 1948, § 13 (3); Commerce Act 1986, § 77 (12); accord, Human Rights Commission Act 1977, § 66 (5).

[108] These figures were obtained from my own worksheets, *supra*, n. 78. The Ryan thesis, *supra*, n. 64, does not indicate the corresponding numbers for 1969–79. The fourteen cases break down as follows: Mr McLauchlan, 6 cases; Mr Frizell, 4 cases; Mr Lyall, 3 cases; and one case in which the entry in the Registry log is illegible and the case file unavailable.

[109] See my worksheets, *supra*, n. 78. There were two lay members in that case: Messrs Neilson and Shaw. Ibid. The same lay members served with Mr Justice Greig in another Commerce Commission case, *Auckland Bulk Gas Users Group* v. *Commerce Comm'n.*, No. M498/87 (heard on several different days in Mar. 1988).

TABLE 5. *Number of Administrative Division Cases Decided by each Judge,[a] 1969–1987*

Judge	Total Admin. Div. cases decided[b]	Years on Admin. Div.	Av. No. per year
Davison, CJ	125	10	12.5
Speight, J.	78	13	6.0
Wild, CJ	75	10	7.5
White, J.	28	9	3.1
Jeffries, J.	26	6	4.3
Casey, J.	25	4	6.3
McMullin, J.	25	4	6.3
Cooke, J.	20	[less than 1]	[more than 20]
Roper, J.	20	4	5.0
Chilwell, J.	19	6	3.2
Wilson, J.	18	4	4.5
Greig, J.	11	2	5.5
Holland, J.	10	3	3.3
Bisson, J.	8	6	1.3
Woodhouse, J.	7	6	1.2
Mahon, J.	5	2	2.5
Tompkins, J.	3	2	1.5
McGregor, J.	0	1	0.0
Doogue, J.	0	1	0.0
Other judges	53	—	—
Totals	556	93	6.0

[a] The figures showing the number of cases decided by each judge are the sums of those for 1969–79, taken from Ryan, *supra*, n. 64, App. IV, Table 7, and those for 1980–7, taken from my worksheets, *supra*, n. 78. They include both appeal and review, and they include those Administrative Division cases that the judges decided before becoming members of the Division. See text accompanying *supra*, nn. 72–3. The figures for number of years served on the Administrative division are taken from Table 4 *supra*. The last column is simply the total cases divided by the years of service.

[b] There is a slight, and unavoidable, inaccuracy here. The number of cases decided from 1969 to 1979 was derived from Ryan, *supra*, n. 64, App. IV, Table 7. That Table combines, under the heading 'Other', those judges who had not yet been named to the Division but who might none the less have decided a small number of Administrative Division cases (see *supra*, nn. 72–3). If any judges in that category were later assigned to the Division, then the information in this column will understate slightly the total number of Division cases decided by those judges.

generally meaningless for those judges whose appointments to the Division are very recent. Moreover, not all Division cases are equal; certain case types are more complex than others. Table 6 will offer more specific information about the distribution of cases by subject-matter.

With those caveats, however, some useful information can be gleaned from these figures. The most obvious conclusion is that, from its inception, the Division has been dominated by a handful of individuals. Chief Justice Davison alone decided 125 of the 334 Administrative Division cases that were decided during his pre-31 December 1987 tenure on the Division.[110] Over the nineteen-year period that the present study encompasses, three judges—Chief Justices Wild and Davison and Mr Justice Speight[111]—collectively decided exactly half the Division's cases. Those three judges are also the ones with the longest periods of service on the Administrative Division, but even when the figures are adjusted to account for longevity, these three members continue to dominate.[112]

The domination theme is reinforced when the distribution of the cases is examined by calendar year. Chief Justice Davison assigned[113] to himself twelve of the twenty-five cases decided in 1985, eight of nineteen in 1986, and eight of twenty-one in 1987—almost as many cases as those he assigned in those years to all the other Division members combined.[114]

Probably even more important than the allocation of the total Administrative Division work-load is the distribution of cases by subject-matter. Table 6 charts the assignments for each of the six

[110] Chief Justice Davison joined the Administrative Division upon his appointment as Chief Justice in 1978. See Chief Justice letter, *supra*, ch. 3 n. 28, Attachment. From 1978 to 1987, the Division decided 334 cases. See *supra*, Table 3, last column.

[111] As Table 5 shows, they decided 278 of the 556 cases.

[112] Among those judges who have served five years or more, these three have the highest number of cases decided per year of service. See the last column of Table 5.

[113] Case assignments are made by the executive judges for the particular circuit. See Chief Justice letter, *supra*, ch. 3 n. 28, para. 6 (f). Administrative Division cases are ordinarily filed at the central registry in Wellington. Administrative Division Rules, *supra*, n. 58, para. 691. Thus, the Chief Justice generally assigns the Division's cases.

[114] These figures were derived from my worksheets, *supra*, n. 78. In 1987, Chief Justice Davison assigned 7 of the remaining 13 cases to Mr Justice Greig. Ibid.

TABLE 6. *Subject-Matter of Cases Decided by Particular Judges*[a] *1969–1987*

Judge	Land Valuation	Planning	Liquor Licensing	Accident Compensation	Sales Tax[b]	Broad-casting	Other subjects[c]	Total
Davison, CJ	12	15	17	12	12	6	51	125
Speight, J.	27	21	5	4	1	6	14	78
Wild, CJ	41	11	11	0	0	3	9	75
White, J.	7	4	7	2	0	1	7	28
Jeffries, J.	1	8	3	1	4	0	9	26
Casey, J.	2	8	2	6	0	0	7	25
McMullin, J.	4	6	11	0	0	0	4	25
Cooke, J.	10	8	1	0	0	0	1	20
Roper, J.	3	10	2	1	1	0	3	20
Chilwell, J.	0	13	2	1	1	0	2	19
Wilson, J.	11	2	4	0	0	1	0	18
Greig, J.	1	4	0	0	0	3	3	11
Holland, J.	1	4	1	0	2	2	0	10
Bisson, J.	0	2	0	3	1	0	2	8
Woodhouse, J.	1	1	4	0	0	0	1	7
Mahon, J.	1	1	1	2	0	0	0	5
Tompkins, J.	0	2	0	1	0	0	0	3
McGregor, J.	0	0	0	0	0	0	0	0
Doogue, J.	0	0	0	0	0	0	0	0
Other judges[d]	13	11	7	6	4	1	11	53
Total	135	131	78	39	26	23	124	556

[a] All figures are derived from Ryan, *supra*, n. 64, App. IV, Table 7, and from my worksheets, *supra*, n. 78. For details, see *supra*, Table 5, n. a. As in Tables 2 and 3, individual subject category figures reflect appeals only; the applications for review are included in the column labelled 'Other subjects'.

[b] Precise figures for 1969–79 are unavailable, but the total number of such cases is negligible. See *supra*, Table 2.

[c] Including applications for review.

[d] See *supra*, Table 5 n. b.

most voluminous case categories. It helps answer two related questions: Has some subject-matter become the nearly exclusive province of one, or perhaps two, judges? And have some judges become single-speciality experts?

As for the former question, a few of the relatively high-volume subject areas do seem to have been captured by one or two judges. Land valuation has comprised the Division's heaviest diet to date, and in that area more than half the cases have been decided by two individuals—Chief Justice Wild and Mr Justice Speight. This fact is striking enough, but it becomes more so when it is considered that the tenures of those judges ended in 1978 and 1982, respectively.[115] Similarly, as Table 6 shows, Chief Justice Davison and Mr Justice Speight together decided more than half the broadcasting cases, and Chief Justice Davison alone decided almost half the sales tax cases.

In the lower volume subjects not covered by Table 6, the dominance of Chief Justice Davison is even more dramatic. From 1980 to 1987[116] he decided ten of the twelve motor vehicle dealers licensing cases; ten of the twelve fisheries cases; five of the seven immigration cases; and all five of the commerce cases.[117]

The converse question concerns the emergence of the highly specialized judge. As Table 6 illustrates, Chief Justice Wild majored in land valuation (forty-one of his seventy-five decisions); he seems to have minored in planning cases and liquor licensing cases (twenty-two of his remaining thirty-four cases). Mr Justice Cooke (as he then was) specialized in land cases; eighteen of his twenty decisions involved either land valuation or planning. Eleven of Mr Justice McMullin's twenty-five decisions were liquor licensing cases. Of Mr Justice Wilson's eighteen cases, eleven were in the area of planning. And Mr Justice Chilwell, whose pre-appointment experience included a fair amount of planning law,[118] has decided thirteen planning cases out of his total Administrative Division case-load of nineteen.

115 See Table 4 *supra*. To be fair, however, one must consider that the volume of land valuation cases has dropped markedly since 1978. See Table 3 *supra*.

116 I chose this period because the Ryan statistics for previous years, see *supra*, n. 64, App. IV, Table 7, do not segregate all of these areas.

117 My worksheets, *supra*, n. 78.

118 Interview with Mr Justice Chilwell, *supra*, ch. 1 n. 7.

4. *A Multiple-Speciality Model in Operation*

The last consideration pertinent here is the geographic distribution of the judges and the cases. At present three Administrative Division judges are based in Wellington, two in Auckland, and one each in Christchurch and Hamilton.[119] It is not possible to determine from the Registry's Administrative Division log precisely how many cases have been heard in each of these and other High Court locations. Since High Court judges travel very infrequently on Administrative Division cases,[120] however, the distribution of cases among particular judges is at least a crude indicator of geographic dispersal. In the first nineteen years of the Administrative Division, then, 285 cases were decided by Administrative Division judges based in Wellington, 157 by those based in Auckland, 53 by those based in Christchurch, 8 by those based in Hamilton, and 53 by non-Administrative Division judges.[121] When the more recent cases are isolated, those proportions do not change dramatically.[122]

3. *Procedure*

Despite the hopes reflected in the PALRC Report,[123] Administrative Division proceedings are generally conducted in a formal, adversarial[124] atmosphere complete with wigged barristers. The specific procedural ingredients are defined not only by the Judicature Act, particular substantive statutes, and the Administrative

119 Chief Justice letter, *supra*, ch. 3 n. 28, para. 6 (a); Interview with the Deputy Registrar, David Mangos, 21 Jan. 1988.

120 Interview with Mr Mangos, *supra*, n. 119. High Court judges travel often on non-Administrative Division cases, since the Court sits in several low-population cities. Ibid.

121 During their tenure on the Administrative Division, the judges were based as follows: in Wellington, Chief Justices Wild and Davison, and Messrs Justices White, Cooke, Jeffries, and Greig; in Auckland, Messrs Justices Woodhouse, Speight, McMullin, Chilwell, Casey, and Tompkins; in Christchurch, Messrs Justices McGregor, Wilson, Mahon, Roper, and Holland; and in Hamilton, Messrs Justices Bisson and Doogue. Telephone Conversation with the Deputy Registrar, David Mangos, 14 June 1988. The figures in the text are the sums of the cases decided by all the Administrative Division judges for a given city; the numbers for the individual judges in turn were taken from Table 5 *supra*.

122 For the 1980–7 period, the methodology described in *supra*, n. 121, produces an estimated 143 decisions by Wellington judges, 62 by Auckland judges, 31 by Christchurch judges and 8 by Hamilton judges. Another 14 cases were decided during this period by judges who were not members of the Administrative Division.

123 See 1968 PALRC Rpt., *supra*, ch. 1 n. 23, para. 36 (v).

124 See Ryan, *supra*, n. 64, at 108.

Division Rules,[125] but also by the judges themselves, who possess wide discretion to tailor the procedure to the needs of the individual cases.[126] As to the latter, my impressions of typical Administrative Division practice are gleaned from a range of sources: interviews with the judges and the Deputy Registrar; examination of case files in the more commonly recurring categories of cases; personal observation of Administrative Division proceedings; tabulations from the Registry log, and, for the older cases, the Ryan statistics; and the published and unpublished Administrative Division judgments.

An Administrative Division case is ordinarily heard by a single judge.[127] The judge has the benefit of a case file that typically contains a fairly detailed administrative record. By some statutes[128] and by the Administrative Division Rules,[129] the tribunal must forward to the court a record that contains all the papers and exhibits that were lodged with the tribunal and, if a factual hearing has been held, any transcribed notes of the evidence. In some of the case files that I examined, the transcript was quite lengthy.[130] The court has the discretion to take new evidence and to retake oral evidence,[131] but in practice those powers are seldom invoked.[132]

[125] See *supra*, n. 58. The Rules do not apply, however, to review proceedings. Administrative Division Rules, 677 (2), 689.

[126] See Administrative Division Rules, *supra*, n. 58, §§ 686, 687, 695, 696 (2, 3, 5, 6), 697.

[127] Judicature Act 1908, § 26 (2); Interview with Mr Mangos, *supra*, n. 119. One exception is the Medical Practitioners Act 1968, § 59A, which requires three-judge panels in appeals from specified disciplinary proceedings for physicians. Another exception, of course, is the use of one or two additional lay members in certain types of cases. See text accompanying *supra*, nn. 100–9.

[128] e.g. Town and Country Planning Act 1977, § 162C; Sale of Liquor Act 1962, §§ 226C, 227 (5).

[129] See *supra*, n. 58, §§ 693, 696.

[130] See esp. *United Broadcasters* v. *Radio Horowhenua*, No. M570/85 (13 Feb. 1987); *Broadcasting Corp. of New Zealand* v. *FM Radio Enterprises*, Nos. M363/82, M364/82 (24 Nov. 1982); *Rouse* v. *Motor Vehicle Dealers Licensing Board*, No. M694/84 (2 Oct. 1985).

[131] See Administrative Division Rules, *supra*, n. 58, § 696 (2, 3).

[132] Chief Justice letter, *supra*, ch. 3 n. 28, para. 5 (b); Interview with Mr Justice Jeffries, *supra*, ch. 1 n. 8; Interview with Mr Justice Holland, *supra*, ch. 1 n. 7. The only case file I examined in which the court admitted new evidence was *Fletcher Metals* v. *Fletcher Trust and Investment Co.*, No. M600/85 (28 Apr. 1986), where an expert witness was cross-examined on statements he had made in his affidavit. One case that I observed was *Auckland Bulk Gas Users Group* v. *Commerce*

4. *A Multiple-Speciality Model in Operation*

On matters of law the court receives guidance from up to four sources: the reasoned explanation normally provided by the tribunal,[133] the notice of appeal,[134] counsel's written submissions to the court,[135] and oral argument. The court may also require the tribunal to lodge a formal report describing the considerations that led to its decision,[136] but again the adequacy of the existing record makes the exercise of this power infrequent.[137]

Comm'n., No. M498/87 (heard on several different days in Mar. 1988), an appeal from the Commerce Commission on an issue concerning the pricing of natural gas. The court there permitted several days of testimony from expert witnesses. The questioning was highly technical and complex, involving problems of depreciation, economic conditions, and investment strategy. The questions were usually, though not always, couched in a manner that would have complied with the formal rules of evidence had they been applicable. During the morning tea break, however, Mr Justice Greig told me that such exhaustive questioning was exceptionally uncommon. He said the only reason it had been necessary in this case was that no evidentiary hearing had been held at the administrative level. Conversation with Mr Justice Greig, 17 Mar. 1988.

133 Interview with Mr Justice Jeffries, *supra*, ch. 1 n. 8; Chief Justice letter, *supra*, ch. 3 n. 28, para. 5 (a). See generally Administrative Division Rules, *supra*, n. 58, § 695. Some statutes either expressly require the furnishing of reasons, e.g., Accident Compensation Act 1982, § 102 (13), or authorize the court to require reasons in individual cases, e.g., Sale of Liquor Act 1962, § 226C. In the case files that I examined, the tribunals supplied reasoned decisions in a broad range of areas: see, e.g., *New Zealand Steel* v. *Commerce Comm'n.*, No. M725/85 (10 June 1986) (commerce); *Fletcher Metals* v. *Fletcher Trust & Investment Co.*, No. M600/85 (28 Apr. 1986) (same); *United Broadcasters* v. *Radio Horowhenua*, No. M570/85 (13 Feb. 1987); *Matter of Wesseling*, No. M409/82 (5 Mar. 1984) (deportation); *Godfrey* v. *Christchurch City Council*, No. M624/85 (9 Jan. 1987) (planning); *Jacobson* v. *Mt. Wellington Borough Council*, No. M82/82 (22 July 1982) (same); *Oliver* v. *Accident Compensation Corp.*, No. M7/85 (27 June 1985) (accident compensation); *Boulevard Holdings* v. *Licensing Control Comm'n.*, No. M324/85 (18 Oct. 1985) (liquor licensing); *Greg Christensen Enterprises* v. *Licensing Control Comm'n.*, No. M481/85 (13 May 1986) (same); *New Zealand Classic Car Co. v. Motor Vehicle Dealers Licensing Bd.*, No. M29/85 (21 Feb. 1985) (dealers licensing); *Rouse* v. *Motor Vehicle Dealers Licensing Bd.*, No. M694/84 (2 Oct. 1985) (same); *Valuer-General* v. *Winchcombe*, No. LVP 13/82 (29 Apr. 1986) (land valuation).

134 The Administrative Division Rules, *supra*, n. 58, § 692 (d), require that the notice of appeal specify the grounds of appeal 'with such reasonable particularity as to give full advice' on the issues.

135 Written submissions are authorized by the Administrative Division Rules, *supra*, n. 58, § 687, and are quite common. They were included in every one of the case files cited in *supra*, n. 133 except *United Broadcasters, Wesseling*, and *Rouse*. They also appeared in one case file that did not contain a reasoned tribunal decision: *Matter of Martin*, No. M271/83 (6 Apr. 1984).

136 Administrative Division Rules, *supra*, n. 58, § 695.

137 Chief Justice letter, *supra*, ch. 3 n. 28, para. 5 (a); Interview with Mr Justice

4. *A Multiple-Speciality Model in Operation*

Disposition speed is difficult to assess. Statistics compiled during the early years of the Division illustrated unusually speedy disposition, a result two writers ascribed to the high priority Chief Justice Wild assigned Administrative Division cases.[138] One of the writers observed a significant increase in delay—both from the parties' notification of readiness to the hearing date, and from the hearing date to final judgment—once Chief Justice Davison took office.[139] As that writer acknowledged, however, changes in the mix of the Court's cases over the period make meaningful comparison problematic.[140] Moreover, it is not obvious that a Chief Justice *should* attach a higher priority to Administrative Division cases than to any other categories. Current tabulations are not readily available.[141] Even if they were, and even if accurate adjustments for subject-matter mix could be made, the figures would at most shed light on the inclinations of particular Chief Justices;[142] they would reveal little about the concept of the Administrative Division and even less about the general merits of multiple-speciality adjudication.

C. AN APPRAISAL[143]

The concept of a special judicial unit to hear appeals from administrative agencies promised excitement but, in the case of the Administrative Division, delivered anticlimax. Try as I might, I could not discover even the germs of a shared enthusiasm over its

Jeffries, *supra*, ch. 1 n. 8. In none of the case files I examined was such a report required.

[138] See Ryan, *supra*, n. 64, at 75–7; ibid., App. IV, Tables 13, 14; Northey, *supra*, n. 65, at 190.

[139] Ryan, *supra*, n. 64, at 76–7; ibid., App. IV, Table 15.

[140] Ibid. at 77.

[141] Chief Justice letter, *supra*, ch. 3 n. 28, para. 7 (b).

[142] Arguably they would not do even that. Post-hearing delay also depends heavily, if not primarily, on the speed of the other Justices. Moreover, even the pre-hearing delay can be affected by the status of the other cases for which the judges are responsible.

[143] As the preceding pages reveal, this study required not only traditional searches of the existing literature, but also interviews and correspondence with all the Justices on the Administrative Division and other knowledgeable individuals, study of various statistical compilations, examination of individual case files, and personal observations of court proceedings. The conclusions are strictly my own except where specified otherwise.

actual operation. None the less, some benefits have derived from it. The obstacles to more striking successes provide valuable lessons about the pitfalls of specialized adjudication and the ways in which to avoid them.

1. *Suitability of Subject-Matter: Why Administrative Law?*

Like the wholly separate court systems of France and other European nations,[144] the existence of the Administrative Division reflects an assumption that there is indeed something different about administrative law. But is there? And if there is, how do the differences affect the case for specialized adjudication?

The various public programmes bound together under the heading of administrative law share several common attributes relevant to the wisdom of consolidating the appellate function within a single specialized forum. First, in a broad sense, they generate a number of common legal issues: When is procedural fairness in adjudication required, and what does it entail when it is? What procedures must administrative bodies follow when they issue rules? What is the scope of judicial review or appeal? Second, certain specific administrative programmes can be grouped in ways that permit frequent use of analogy: some programmes establish professional licensing systems, others are concerned with welfare benefits, still others with the regulation of industry.

Some have suggested that administrative law is also distinguished by a propensity to raise questions of social and economic policy.[145] Of this I am not so convinced. Certain kinds of administrative law cases surely have that tendency; the economic judgments vital in many trade regulation cases come immediately to mind. But others—accident compensation, land valuation, and other cases so often characterized by repetitive questions of fact—do not seem unusually likely to implicate fundamental

[144] See *supra*, Intro., n. 5.

[145] e.g. 1965 Orr Lecture, *supra*, Intro., n. 5, at 12; 1968 PALRC Rpt., *supra*, ch. 1 n. 23, Minority View of G. S. Orr, App., para. 3 (c); Interview with Rt. Hon. Sir Robin Cooke, *supra*, ch. 1 n. 30; Interview with Mr Justice Holland, *supra*, ch. 1 n. 7.

policy. Conversely, private law areas can raise policy questions with equal facility; the common law development of products liability in tort, unconscionability doctrine in contract, and intestate succession rules in property law are only a few examples. It is true that these private law policy determinations do not generally require the balancing of individual and governmental interests,[146] but that kind of balancing is present in such other public law areas as criminal justice and constitutional law. Further, while the need to safeguard the individual from unwarranted governmental intrusion is a classic explanation for entrusting the review function to a forum with the status and independence of a court,[147] the fact that the conflict pits the individual against the government is not of obvious relevance to the question whether the reviewing court should be specialized.

Application of the previously developed general criteria for specialized adjudication[148] exposes the difficulty of viewing administrative law monolithically for present purposes. The proportions of legal, factual, and discretionary decisions range widely from one administrative programme to another. In the Administrative Division itself, the planning appeals on questions of law[149] can be contrasted with the fact questions that typify the land valuation cases.[150] As the preceding discussion shows, the prevalence of policy questions also differs enormously among the various programmes.

The same is true of the degree of technicality, one of the more important criteria for specialization. The issues presented in welfare cases, or in liquor licence cases, do not often pose the kinds of technical problems that surface so frequently in economically technical trade cases, or scientifically technical patent cases, or financially technical securities cases.

[146] This feature of administrative law was noted by the Rt. Hon. Sir Robin Cooke, *supra*, ch. 1 n. 30.

[147] e.g. L. L. Jaffe, *English and American Judges as Lawmakers*, 32–3 (1969); Lord Hailsham, 'The Lord Chancellor and Judicial Independence', 11 *Cambrian L. Rev.* 40 (1980).

[148] See *supra*, ch. 2.

[149] Planning appeals are statutorily restricted to questions of law. Town and Country Planning Act 1977, § 162.

[150] As noted earlier, *supra*, n. 108 and accompanying text, lay members have sat in fourteen of the last eighteen land valuation cases. They do not sit when the issues are legal. Land Valuation Proceedings Act 1948, § 13 (4) (d).

Nor can administrative law fairly be described as an isolated area in which the benefits of a generalist perspective are unimportant. Issues of procedural fairness are not peculiar to administrative justice; they arise in other civil cases and in criminal cases as well. So, too, do issues as to the standard of review.

Administrative cases also vary considerably by the extent of repetition. Social security disability cases in the United States, turning as they so often do on the sufficiency of the evidence supporting the finding of ability to work,[151] can be expected to produce far greater repetition than, say, the more varied issues presented in planning cases or commercial cases. The same can be said of degree of controversy and degree of clannishness; both vary significantly from one programme to another.

The degree to which consistency is important also distinguishes some administrative programmes from others. Consistency is of course desirable generally. Even in accident compensation cases or land valuation cases, perceptions of disparity can hinder public acceptance of either the substantive programme or the adjudicative forum. But in some areas of administrative law consistency assumes special importance. In liquor licensing cases, for example, consistency is particularly crucial because applicants can be competitors.[152]

Another specialization criterion dependent on the particular administrative programme is the rapidity of change. The issues presented in planning and environmental cases, for example, are influenced by such rapidly changing factors as the economy, the state of technology, and the discovery of new environmental dangers. In other areas, the pace of change may be slower.

Volume is one of the more obvious differences among the various administrative schemes. In New Zealand, however, even the total volume of the Administrative Division's cases is low enough to thwart the attainment of significant benefits. This problem is addressed separately below.[153]

Finally, the remaining specialization criteria—the importance of a prompt decision and the existence of special procedural needs at the appellate level—similarly defy attempts to generalize to administrative law. Land valuation cases, for example, might well

[151] 42 USC § 1382c (a) (3).

[152] See *supra*, ch. 2, § B. 8.

[153] See *infra*, § 3.

require the special procedure that has been devised.[154] And in those cases in which individuals retain the benefits of the status quo while their litigation is pending, and therefore possess an incentive to file frivolous actions to achieve delay, speedy disposition brings special benefits.[155] These kinds of considerations are at most programme-specific, not endemic to administrative law.

As the above discussion demonstrates, then, the case attributes that ordinarily favour specialized adjudication are far more prevalent in some administrative programmes than they are in others. The existence of general administrative law principles is a significant unifying factor, but that factor seems overshadowed by the substantive programmatic differences and their effects on the general criteria for specialization. It follows that, ideally, not all administrative decisions should be forced into the same appellate mould. In the case of the Administrative Division, where the volumes are extremely low and many of the specific jurisdictional grants seem well suited to specialization, the imprecision is probably not important enough to warrant a time-consuming, programme-by-programme evaluation. But the variations described here leave me unpersuaded that administrative law, undifferentiated, is in general a suitable candidate for a specialized appellate unit.

With all that, the strongest reason to retain the Administrative Division might be a tactical one. A specialized High Court division, it will be recalled, was the vehicle by which the original PALRC Report reconciled its preference for appeals to the Supreme Court (now the High Court) with its concern about judges' relative lack of expertise and interest in administrative law.[156] Abolition of the Administrative Division, therefore, could strip the High Court of its appellate jurisdiction; administrative tribunals could become the final appellate authorities. That prospect seems unlikely, since judges are more interested in, and more informed about, administrative law today than they were in 1968.[157] Consequently, the case for permitting appeal to the High

[154] Land Valuation Proceedings Act 1948, § 13.

[155] See Legomsky, *supra*, Intro., n. 8, at 1330–2.

[156] See *supra*, text accompanying nn. 39–43. Accord, Interview with Mr Justice Chilwell, *supra*, ch. 1 n. 7.

[157] Interviews with Rt. Hon. Sir Robin Cooke, *supra*, ch. 1 n. 30, and Mr Justice Jeffries, *supra*, ch. 1 n. 8. Mr Justice Jeffries added that, apart from judges'

Court does not now rest as heavily on the existence of a specialized division. But not everyone would regard the abolition of High Court appeals with alarm, a point beyond the scope of this work.[158] Thus, to the extent that the preservation of High Court appeals is independently desirable, the retention of the Administrative Division has strategic benefit.

2. *Quality of Decisions*

I have read a vast number of the Administrative Division's judgments, in a broad cross-section of cases. Impressions of quality are of course highly subjective. With respect, I have found the craftsmanship generally in keeping with the Court's usual high standards, a reaction shared by the Royal Commission on the Courts in its 1978 study.[159] I cannot truthfully say the quality appeared superior to the Court's general norms, but it might be that the technical difficulties of some of the subject-matter would have created problems that the Administrative Division judges, through their familiarity, were quietly able to avoid. Possibly too, insights that are currently imperceptible will bear fruit later by clarifying the law and thus reducing future litigation. There is no way to be sure.

Chief Justice Davison expressed the view that the existence of the Division has aided consistency 'to a considerable extent'.[160] My own examination of the cases confirms that impression; I could locate no obvious inconsistencies. The judges' own practices seem to contribute to this enhanced coherence. The two Administrative Division judges based in Auckland told me they often

enhanced interest in administrative law, the need for special judicial expertise has also been lessened by the Judicature Amendment Act 1972, which sapped the subject of much of its mystery. See *supra*, n. 29 and accompanying text.

[158] Among those who would generally prefer not to allow appeals from administrative bodies to the High Court are Mr Justice Holland and Professor Orr. See Interviews, *supra*, ch. 1 n. 7 and this ch. n. 95. Mr Justice Holland, however, emphasized that supervisory review should remain a High Court responsibility, and that if, despite this preference, the High Court retains its appellate jurisdiction, then the Administrative Division should probably be retained also to promote consistency in administrative policy.

[159] *Supra*, ch. 1 n. 30, para. 312 (d) ('the successful operation of the Administrative Division to date has demonstrated how well the judges are able to cope with the problems').

[160] Chief Justice letter, *supra*, ch. 3 n. 28, para. 1.

discuss Division cases with each other.[161] Mr Justice Holland identified two respects in which the existence of the Administrative Division has affected his decisions: He sticks especially close to precedent when deciding Division cases, and, when a Division case requires a policy decision, he is more prone than usual to choose a policy that the other Division members are likely to find agreeable over a policy that reflects his own preferences.[162]

Previous writers have found in the Division's judgments a general pattern of deference to the administrative authority whose decision was being appealed.[163] The Division seems particularly inclined to defer to the factual inferences drawn by administrative tribunals.[164] I share those impressions and take no position here on the appropriate degree of judicial deference to tribunals with specialized expertise.[165]

3. *Impact of Low Volumes*

Of the seven then current Administrative Division members and the other knowledgeable individuals to whom I posed the question,[166] only one thought the Division had realized, to any considerable extent, the objectives for which it was created. Several reasons were offered.[167] The overwhelming sentiment is

[161] Interviews with Messrs Justices Chilwell and Tompkins, *supra*, ch. 1 n. 7.

[162] Interview with Mr Justice Holland, *supra*, ch. 1 n. 7.

[163] Ryan, *supra*, n. 64, at 87 (planning and liquor licensing), 93 (broadcasting), 95–7 (film licensing); Northey, *supra*, n. 65, at 190–1.

[164] See esp. Ryan, *supra*, n. 64, at 96–7. See also *United Broadcasters* v. *Radio Horowhenua*, No. M570/85 (13 Feb. 1987) (deferring to expert conclusion of Broadcasting Tribunal that particular music would cater to particular audience).

[165] I have examined this question elsewhere. See Legomsky *supra*, ch. 3 n. 1, ch. 5.

[166] Interviews with Rt. Hon. Sir Robin Cooke, *supra*, ch. 1 n. 30, Sir Kenneth Keith, Deputy President, New Zealand Law Commn., 18 Jan. 1988, and Professor Orr, *supra*, n. 95. Five of the seven Division members responded orally. See Interviews, *supra*, ch. 1 nn. 7, 8. Chief Justice Davison preferred to respond in writing. See *supra*, ch. 3 n. 28. I was unable to travel to Hamilton to interview Mr Justice Doogue, who had been recently appointed to the Division and who had decided no Division cases as of 31 Dec. 1987, but he kindly provided his views in writing. Letter from Mr Justice Doogue, 17 May 1988.

[167] Professor Orr had the more fundamental objection that appeals from administrative bodies should ordinarily be heard by a separate Administrative Court rather than by a division of the High Court. Interview with Professor Orr, *supra*, n. 95. That view is expressed more fully in his writing. See 1964 Orr Rpt., *supra*, Intro., n. 3; 1965 Orr Lecture, *supra*, Intro., n. 5; 1968 PALRC Rpt., *supra*, ch. 1 n. 23, App. (Minority View of G. S. Orr). Mr Justice Holland believed that

that the chief culprit has been the small case-load, which has stunted the growth of expertise and in many instances has thwarted even basic familiarity.[168] Mr Justice Holland put the point succinctly: 'How does one acquire expertise in broadcasting law from two cases?'[169]

The one respondent who believed the Division had achieved its objectives 'to a considerable extent' was Chief Justice Davison.[170] Significantly, he was the only then current member to have decided a massive number of Administrative Division cases.[171] That the only member with a heavy Division case-load sensed the emergence of expertise while the others did not is scarcely surprising.

To say that a specialized division cannot succeed without a sufficient case-load is to state the obvious. The reactions of the then current Administrative Division judges seem to confirm that their Division case-loads, with the exception of Chief Justice Davison's, are simply not sufficient to trigger the benefits of specialization. This problem could not be cured by distributing the Division's work more uniformly among its members even if there were no geographic barriers to doing this. Twenty-nine cases per year[172] divided equally among the seven members of the Division would produce a total Division case-load of about four cases per year per member in all fields of administrative activity combined–hardly enough to inspire significant expertise. If the

appeals from administrative bodies are generally best handled by administrative tribunals. He acknowledged that judicial review belongs in the High Court, but suggested that it does not require specialized judges. He therefore saw no need for an Administrative Division, though he would prefer to retain it if the High Court retains its appellate jurisdiction. Interview with Mr Justice Holland, *supra*, ch. 1 n. 7. Mr Justice Jeffries considered the Division dispensable because the Judicature Amendment Act 1972 and other developments have drained administrative law of the mysticism that once necessitated special expertise. Interview with Mr Justice Jeffries, *supra*, ch. 1 n. 8.

[168] In addition to the interviews of the Division members and the individuals listed in *supra*, n. 166, see 1980 PALRC Rpt., *supra*, ch. 1 n. 17, para. 18; Ryan, *supra*, n. 64, at 104, 106; cf. Northey, *supra*, n. 65, at 187–9 (noting the surprisingly small number of cases).

[169] Interview with Mr Justice Holland, *supra*, ch. 1 n. 7. That is the number he had decided in his three years on the Division. See *supra*, Tables 4, 6.

[170] Chief Justice letter, *supra*, ch. 3 n. 28.

[171] See *supra*, Tables 5 and 6. See generally *supra*, § B. 2.

[172] See *supra*, Table 2 and text accompanying n. 80. Even the figure of 29 is probably high. In the last three years studied, the average annual case-load of the Division was only 22. See *supra*, Table 3.

Division is retained—and whether it should be is considered in the conclusion to this chapter—ways in which to increase the number of Division cases per member should therefore be examined.

Expanding the jurisdiction of the Division is one possible response, but that course of action would not solve the basic problem. First, most of the major administrative decisions are already appealable to the Division. With the exception of certain transport licensing cases,[173] there is little left to add. Second, for the reasons given in subsection 1, it is specific individual programmes, not administrative law generally, that benefit from judicial specialization. Adding a new category of Administrative Division jurisdiction might well aid the informed and efficient resolution of those new cases, but it would enhance only marginally the expertise that the members of the Division bring to existing cases. Finally, any decision to expand the jurisdiction of the High Court potentially exacerbates the burdens experienced by a bench that, in the opinion of the President of the Court of Appeal, is already overworked.[174]

An alternative solution might be to reduce the number of Administrative Division members so that each remaining member would have a more substantial exposure to the Division's cases. Although the existing size resulted from an increase that had been recommended by both the Royal Commission on the Courts[175] and the Law Society,[176] this larger size was recently cited as a partial explanation for the relatively low degree of actual specialization.[177]

Yet there would be costs in reducing the size of the Division.

[173] The PALRC continually urged that appeals from various decisions concerning licences for transporting goods and passengers be channelled to the Administrative Division. See PALRC, *Twelfth Report*, para. 8 (1978); PALRC, *Seventh Report, Administrative Tribunals Constitution, Procedure and Appeals*, paras. 9–11 (1974). See also Ryan, *supra*, n. 64, at 56–7; Northey, *supra*, n. 65, at 42. Also mentioning transport as a possible addition were Sir Kenneth Keith, *supra*, n. 166, and Professor Orr, *supra*, n. 95.

[174] Interview with Rt. Hon. Sir Robin Cooke, *supra*, ch. 1 n. 30.

[175] 1978 Royal Commn. Rpt., *supra*, ch. 1 n. 23, at 97, Rec. No. 2; ibid. at 345, Rec. No. 16.

[176] First Submissions of NZ Law Society, *supra*, ch. 1 n. 6, para. 6. 35; NZ Law Society Recs., *supra*, n. 71, para. 21.

[177] Interview with Rt. Hon. Sir Robin Cooke, *supra*, ch. 1 n. 30.

One concern is logistics. It is beneficial to have Division members on hand in the major population centres.[178] Auckland and Wellington certainly each require the permanent attention of at least one Administrative Division judge. Over the studied lifetime of the Division, these cities averaged approximately seven and fifteen Administrative Division cases per year, respectively.[179] Given unpredictable fluctuations, and given also that the Chief Justice's administrative responsibilities could prevent self-assignment of a pressing case, the importance of a second Wellington-based member is apparent.

The logistics could probably be accommodated by those three judgeships alone. Christchurch is a major population centre, but surprisingly it has averaged only about three Division cases per year.[180] Its needs could be met by occasional travel. The same is true of Hamilton. No Administrative Division judge was based there before 1981,[181] and since that time only eight Division cases have been decided by Hamilton-based members.[182] Of course, by the same reasoning, stationing additional members of the Division in these low-volume cities does no real harm. It has little effect at all on the other members' exposure to, and expertise in, the Division's cases.

Despite the absence of a logistical need for seven Administrative Division judges, however, I would not support a significant reduction. To allocate almost all the High Court's administrative law cases to a group of three or four individuals would pose serious institutional dangers. There are hazards in concentrating within so small a group the power to create a vast body of binding law. Apart from the loss of diverse ideas in the development of legal doctrine, there is always the danger, particularly in the many fields of law in which subjective value-judgments are common and unavoidable, that a given area will be shaped almost exclus-

[178] The need for local hearing of cases was emphasized by both Mr Justice Holland and Mr Justice Tompkins. Interviews, *supra*, Intro., n. 7.

[179] To obtain these figures, I simply divided 19 into the total number of cases decided by judges based in these three cities. See *supra*, nn. 119–22 and accompanying text.

[180] Ibid.

[181] Telephone conversation with Mr Mangos, *supra*, n. 121.

[182] As of the end of 1987, Mr Justice Bisson had decided eight, and Mr Justice Doogue none. See *supra*, Table 5 and *supra*, n. 121 and accompanying text.

ively by the ideologies of one or two dominant figures. I am aware of no evidence that that has occurred yet in New Zealand, but no one can predict the substantive viewpoints, the role conceptions, the degree of dogmatism, or the personalities of future High Court judges.

That leaves me, unfortunately, with no solution to the problem of low volume. As the above discussion shows, finding significant additional jurisdiction would be difficult, and reducing the number of Division members would be easy but unhealthy. My own view is that, if the Division is to continue, the low volume is, realistically, a problem that will simply have to be tolerated. It is unavoidable in a country like New Zealand where the population is both small and dispersed.[183] Whether the same arrangement and the same problems would occur elsewhere is a question that the last chapter will address.

4. *Appointment of Division Members*

From the start, the method of selecting Administrative Division members has been controversial. The original PALRC Report recommended they be appointed by the Governor-General, and in this view the Law Society later concurred.[184] But Parliament, seeking to avoid possible future charges of political influence,[185] empowered the Chief Justice to assign High Court judges to the Administrative Division.[186] The then Chief Justice (Wild, CJ) preferred that approach as a method of assuring judicial independence.[187] Chief Justice Davison also approved, but for the different reason that the Chief Justice 'knows the abilities of the various Judges'.[188]

[183] See ch. 5, § B.

[184] 1968 PALRC Rpt., *supra*, ch. 1 n. 23, para. 36 (i); NZ Law Society Recs., *supra*, n. 71, para. 21.

[185] See the comments of the Minister of Justice, 356 *NZ Parl. Debates* 1067, 1068, 35th Parl., 2nd Sess. (6 Aug. 1968); see also A. Paterson, 'First Report of the Public and Administrative Law Reform Committee (Judicature Amendment Act 1968)', 3 *N.Z.U.L. Rev.* 351, 357 (1969).

[186] Judicature Act 1908, § 25 (2).

[187] Wild, *supra*, n. 25, at 263–4.

[188] Chief Justice letter, *supra*, ch. 3 n. 28, para. 6 (c). An intermediate view, taken by the Royal Commission on the Courts, is that the Chief Justice should assign the members but on the recommendation of the Judicial Commission. 1978 Royal Comm'n. Rpt., *supra*, ch. 1 n. 23, para. 312 (b).

With respect, I find the proffered advantages of Chief Justice appointment unconvincing. The second PALRC Report, commenting on Parliament's rejection of the committee's original recommendation, observed that the Governor-General, who would act on the advice of Ministers, is also well suited to assess one's qualifications for Division membership.[189] As for the argument that assignment by the Governor-General might be seen as political, the committee noted that there is no more reason to fear politically motivated decisions to assign members of the Administrative Division than there is to fear politically motivated decisions to appoint High Court judges generally.[190] Chief Justice Wild responded by distinguishing the latter decisions as permanent, at least until the mandatory retirement age.[191] Although he did not elaborate, his point appears to be that the members of the Division should be able to approach cases free of the fear that an unpopular decision could result in their transfer from the Division. The argument has theoretical appeal, but such a threat seems unrealistic and in any event could as easily exist when *any* individual with strongly held views—Governor-General or Chief Justice—has the power to remove members from the Division.

Apart from the absence of significant advantage, the totality of the Chief Justice's powers over the Administrative Division seems to be an affirmative disadvantage. As discussed earlier, in addition to assigning the members themselves, the Chief Justice may assign non-Administrative Division cases to the Division and may divert Administrative Division cases to non-Division judges.[192] And in all these cases, the Chief Justice chooses the judge who will hear the case.[193] This discretion is subject to some practical constraints such as location, but the overwhelming majority of the Division's cases are heard in Wellington and Auckland, where the Chief Justice has, respectively, three and two members from whom to choose.[194] A Chief Justice who wishes to do so could quite easily assign a case on which he or she holds strong views to the Division

[189] PALRC, *Second Report, Appeals from Administrative Tribunals*, para. 6 (1969).

[190] Ibid.

[191] Wild, *supra*, n. 25, at 263–4.

[192] See *supra*, nn. 65–73 and accompanying text.

[193] See *supra*, n. 113 and accompanying text.

[194] See *supra*, nn. 119–22 and accompanying text.

member most likely to decide the issues in a particular way. If the case is to be heard in Wellington, and most are,[195] the Chief Justice could accomplish the same purpose even more efficiently by self-assignment.

Without in any way suggesting anything but the most proper and commendable motives of the two individuals who served as Chief Justice during the studied lifetime of the Administrative Division, I submit, with respect, that this package of sweeping powers threatens both the rule of law and the appearance of justice. As to the former, my fear is confined to the future and to the uncertainty it holds.

5. *Use of Division Members*

My concerns about the distribution of cases among Division members stem partly from the same distrust of concentrated power and partly from the drawbacks of excessively refined specialization. As shown earlier, certain judges have dominated certain categories of cases, and certain case categories have dominated the Division work of certain judges.[196] There admittedly are benefits in that approach; heightening the degree of specialization arguably furthers the goals of expertise, consistency, and efficiency. But there are serious dangers as well. For the same reasons that underlie my opposition to reducing the number of Division members,[197] I would favour a policy of spreading out both the total Division case-load and the various case types among the Division members more uniformly than is the present practice. And for the same reasons that lead me to prefer the multiple speciality model over a single speciality model,[198] I would urge more varied diets of Administrative Division cases for individual members.

Finally, the judges' generally positive comments about the lay members of the Administrative Division should be recorded.[199]

[195] See *supra*, n. 121 and accompanying text.

[196] See *supra*, § B. 2.

[197] See *supra*, text immediately following paragraph containing n. 182.

[198] See *supra*, ch. 3, § B.

[199] Chief Justice Davison found the lay members 'invaluable in both the valuation and commerce fields'. Chief Justice letter, *supra*, ch. 3 n. 28, para. 2 (a). See also Davison, *supra*, n. 22, at 285 (encouraging greater use of expert assessors in cases presenting technical issues). Messrs Justices Jeffries, Holland, and Greig also consider the presence of lay members helpful. Interviews, *supra*, ch. 1 nn. 7, 8.

Chief Justice Davison emphasized both their ability to explain technical matters and their market experience.[200] Mr Justice Holland felt they help him understand the facts, provide insights into the reputations of expert witnesses, serve as sounding-boards for discussion, aid in sorting out the issues, and, by their presence, encourage counsel to assure the correctness of their submissions.[201] None of the judges whose views I solicited thought that judges tended to accord unwarranted deference to the views of the lay members. Two judges said they defer somewhat to the experts' factual conclusions on technical matters, but emphasized that judges ultimately reach their own conclusions.[202] Chief Justice Davison gave 'due weight' to the experts' opinions, but withheld 'blind acceptance'.[203]

6. *Conclusions on the Administrative Division*

The paucity of praise for the Administrative Division can probably be attributed to several factors. Some believe appeals from administrative bodies simply should not go to the High Court at all.[204] Even if appeals to the High Court are taken as a given, there are reasons to be dissatisfied with the creation of a specialized Administrative Division. The low volume seems the most significant barrier to greater achievement.[205] Judges' increased interest in, and knowledge of, administrative law has reduced the need for specialization.[206] And, as examined earlier,[207] the treatment of administrative law as a monolithic discipline has prevented any serious attempt to distinguish those administrative schemes that would thrive on the attention of specialized judges from those that would not.

The remaining members either have never sat with lay members or have done so too infrequently to generalize, Interviews with Messrs Justices Chilwell and Tompkins, *supra*, ch. 1 n. 7, although Mr Justice Doogue questioned, tentatively, the fairness of there being members who represent specialist viewpoints not known to the litigants. Letter from Mr Justice Doogue, *supra*, n. 166.

[200] Chief Justice letter, *supra*, ch. 3 n. 28, para. 2 (a).

[201] Interview with Mr Justice Holland, *supra*, ch. 1 n. 7.

[202] Interviews with Messrs Justices Holland and Greig, *supra*, ch. 1 n. 7. The latter emphasized judges' own experience in finding facts from evidence.

[203] Chief Justice letter, *supra*, ch. 3 n. 28, para. 2 (c).

[204] See *supra*, n. 167.

[205] See *supra*, nn. 168–9.

[206] e.g. Interviews with Rt. Hon. Sir Robin Cooke, *supra*, ch. 1 n. 30, and Mr Justice Jeffries, *supra*, ch. 1 n. 8.

[207] *Supra*, § 1.

4. *A Multiple-Speciality Model in Operation*

The Administrative Division has not produced any earth-shaking benefits, but I believe it has spawned a few minor advantages that probably warrant its retention. The creation of a multiple-speciality adjudicative unit is conceptually sound and should be encouraged. Although administrative law does not fit to an ideal level of purity the general specialization criteria developed earlier, many of the specific administrative programmes within the Division's jurisdiction are in fact reasonably well suited for specialized adjudication. Those that lack the attributes I have associated with specialization probably have not suffered from inclusion, since the reality is that all the members of the Division spend the vast majority of their court time on their general case-loads anyway. Consequently, there is no measurable loss of the generalist perspective.

In addition a handful of judges have become especially knowledgeable about a few of the programmes over which the Division has jurisdiction, partly through longevity and partly through patterns of case assignments. There is some sentiment that moderately enhanced familiarity with a few key programmes has had at least slightly positive effects on the quality and consistency of the judgments and the speed and efficiency of the process. Finally, the Administrative Division remains a useful device for assuring that appeals from administrative bodies lie with the High Court rather than with a complex of administrative tribunals.

There are future dangers in retaining the Administrative Division, but they would be easy to eliminate. My major concern has been the future potential for abuse of power. Like others, I agree with the PALRC Report that the power to assign the members of the Administrative Division should rest with the Governor-General rather than with the Chief Justice. A more uniform distribution of the number and types of Division cases to the various members, to the extent geography permits, would also be beneficial. More equitable sharing will not solve the problem of low volume, and it will cut somewhat into the development of isolated expertise, but it will address both the danger of concentrated power and the deficiencies of unduly narrow specialization.

5

The Inter-Nation Variables

As the preceding chapter illustrates, the success of a specialized adjudication system can depend on certain properties of the country in which it is located. This chapter identifies and discusses some of those inter-nation variables. To keep the analysis within manageable bounds, I shall focus on the relevant differences between two countries—New Zealand and the United States. As will be seen, however, the discussion that follows enlists considerations that are of logical relevance to most modern democracies. The variables fall into two groups: those pertaining to the legal system and the system of government, and those pertaining to population and geography.

A. GOVERNMENT AND LEGAL SYSTEM

New Zealand and the United States share a number of attributes. Both are democracies. Both recognize the principle of separation of powers, though in different ways considered below.[1] Both have independent, secure judiciaries.[2] Both employ English common law traditions, including the practice of following precedent.[3] In the area of administrative justice, both systems rely heavily on a network of specialized administrative tribunals whose decisions are generally subject to some form of judicial scrutiny.[4]

But these similarities mask some important differences. Perhaps the most fundamental concerns primacy. The supremacy of the

[1] See *infra*, nn. 10–32 and accompanying text.

[2] See Palmer, *supra*, ch. 4 n. 3, at 183–4. The judges of the High Court are virtually insulated from removal, Constitution Act 1986, § 23, and from salary reductions, ibid. § 24.

[3] In *Howley* v. *Lawrence Publishing Co.* [1986] NZLR 404, the Court of Appeal voted 3–2 to reserve the right to overrule its own precedents in appropriate cases. See judgments of Woodhouse, P. and Richardson and McMullin, JJ.

[4] See generally Keith, *supra*, ch. 4 n. 22.

United States Constitution[5] contrasts with the supremacy of the New Zealand Parliament.[6] At present, New Zealand has no written constitution. The statutory Constitution Act 1986 lays out the basic structure of the New Zealand government, but Parliament could repeal or amend this legislation at any time.[7]

The existence of an entrenched written constitution in the United States has meant that judges must spend significant proportions of their time defining the scope of the constitutional guarantees. That is a job that calls for legal generalists. Apart from the affirmative value of the generalist perspective, the broad language in which a long-term constitution is necessarily couched leaves much room for the invocation and application of personal values. In that environment, the biases associated with narrow specialization are particularly dangerous.[8] That constitutional issues are often controversial magnifies those dangers.[9] Thus, there exists in the United States an added reason to resist narrowly specialized adjudication systems. The force of that reason rests, of course, on the frequency with which the particular subject-matter raises issues of constitutional stature.

Equally fundamental distinctions between the two systems of government concern their methods of achieving separation of powers. The New Zealand system, based on the Westminster model, is characterized by an extremely close relationship between Parliament and the executive. All the ministers are members of Parliament.[10] Caucuses composed of each party's members of

[5] *Marbury* v. *Madison*, 5 US (1 Cranch) 137 (1803).

[6] See Palmer, *supra*, ch. 4 n. 3, at 186–9; see also *Fitzgerald* v. *Muldoon* [1976] 2 NZLR 615 (English Bill of Rights 1688 prohibits executive branch of New Zealand government from interfering with Parliament).

[7] See Palmer, *supra*, ch. 4 n. 3, at 214–15. The Labour government issued a White Paper, *A Bill of Rights for New Zealand* (1985), in which it recommended an entrenched Bill of Rights. The intention then was to defer introduction of an actual bill until the emergence of a public consensus in favour of it, see White Paper at 5; at present, such a consensus seems unlikely. In 1988, however, a select committee authorized by Parliament issued a report recommending non-entrenched legislation that would embody various individual rights. See *Final Report of the Justice and Law Reform Committee on a White Paper on a Bill of Rights for New Zealand* (1988). The then Minister of Justice (now Prime Minister) expressed support for the committee's recommendations. Press Statement, Rt. Hon. Geoffrey Palmer, 4 Oct. 1988.

[8] See text accompanying *supra*, ch. 1 nn. 28–34.

[9] See *supra*, ch. 2, § B. 6.

[10] Constitution Act 1986, § 6.

Parliament elect the party leaders and deputy leaders; in this way, the caucus of the majority party in Parliament elects the Prime Minister, the Deputy Prime Minister, and, in the case of the Labour Party, the rest of the Cabinet as well.[11]

But the overriding reality of the New Zealand system is that the Cabinet drives Parliament, not vice versa. All major decisions are made by Cabinet, and it is a Cabinet minister who ordinarily introduces bills.[12] All bills must be cleared by caucus, but a united Cabinet ordinarily has little difficulty prevailing in caucus.[13] The members of Parliament are either formally pledged to support the position of their party's caucus or bound in practice to do so; this tight party discipline makes it 'very rare indeed for MPs to cross the floor of the House'.[14] And once Parliament votes, only the virtually pro forma royal assent is required before the bill becomes law.[15] Consequently, executive proposals are rarely defeated.

The United States system stands in stark contrast. Party discipline is much less stringent, and an independently elected President can in any event be of a different political party from the majority of Congress.[16] Moreover, the possibility of a Presidential veto[17] invites a greater chance of confrontation between the legislative and executive branches.

In some ways, the closeness of the two political branches in New Zealand, combined with the realities of party discipline and executive dominance, fortify the case for specialized adjudication. One effect of the New Zealand arrangement is that the law changes rapidly.[18] Dynamics favour specialization.[19] Another effect is that administrative agencies within the executive branch tend to be given a wider ranging discretion than their American counterparts.[20] As discussed earlier, subject-matter characterized

[11] Palmer, *supra*, ch. 4 n. 3, at 8, 72.

[12] Ibid. at 38.

[13] Ibid. at 8, 70–1. Apart from the effects of party discipline, the Cabinet typically comprises one-third to one-half of the caucus members, and the Cabinet members tend to be the more experienced members. Ibid. at 10.

[14] Ibid. at 70–1.

[15] Ibid. at 28–9.

[16] US Const. art. II, § 1, cl. 2 (President technically chosen by 'electors' who are now themselves popularly elected).

[17] Ibid., art. I, § 7, para. 2.

[18] See Palmer, *supra*, ch. 4 n. 3, ch. 9 ('The Fastest Law in the West').

[19] See *supra*, ch. 2, § B. 9.

[20] See Palmer, *supra*, ch. 4 n. 3, at 165–70 (illustrating the breadth of the powers exercised by regulation; certain such powers have since been narrowed).

by a high proportion of discretionary judgments will often be handled best by specialized adjudicators at the initial stages, though by generalists at the appellate level.[21] But in my view the effect with the greatest importance to the present discussion is the enormity of the executive authority. Some degree of substantive familiarity with individual programmes endows the adjudicative body with the knowledge and perhaps the confidence to provide a genuine check.

While New Zealand's executive branch possesses far greater power than its American counterpart, the power *within* the New Zealand executive is more dispersed and subject to more extensive checks. One of the important checks is the principle of collective Cabinet responsibility. As the then Deputy Prime Minister put it, 'No votes are taken in Cabinet. Discussion proceeds until there is a clear consensus.'[22] Moreover, once the Cabinet reaches its decision, all Cabinet members share the responsibility for it and none is permitted to disagree publicly.[23]

A further check within New Zealand's executive branch is the related principle of individual ministerial responsibility. Every minister is individually accountable for actions taken by the employees of his or her departments.[24] In contrast, the only elected officials in the executive branch of the United States are the President and the Vice-President;[25] thus, except for the President, there is no elected official who is accountable for the actions of specific executive agencies.

For those reasons, the executive power in New Zealand is relatively dispersed. That dispersal is an effective counterbalance to the overall potency of the executive branch. Therefore, although I have cited the breadth of the executive power as an argument for deploying specialized adjudicators to assure more searching review in individual cases, the internal checks described above militate in the opposite direction.

Within the legislative branch, however, New Zealand has fewer checks than does the United States. The unicameral New Zealand

21 See *supra*, ch. 2, § B. 1.
22 Palmer, *supra*, ch. 4 n. 3, at 40.
23 Ibid. at 45.
24 Ibid. at 46–7.
25 US Const. art. II, § 1; ibid., amends. XII, XX.

Parliament[26] contrasts with the bicameral United States Congress.[27] And the virtually automatic assent of the Governor-General in New Zealand[28] contrasts with the realistic prospects of Presidential vetoes in the United States. In both respects, the American legislative process is characterized by greater dispersal of power, and more internal scrutiny, than the New Zealand legislative process.

There are differences within the judicial branch as well. On the one hand, American judges have law clerks capable of careful legal research that can reduce the need for specialized judicial expertise. On the other hand, law clerks can perform another function that reduces one of the dangers of specialized adjudication. In the Court of Appeals for the Ninth Circuit, for example, one duty of the central legal staff has been the preliminary screening of cases for assessments of complexity.[29] The staff attorneys identify the main issues, and assign cases numerical weights intended as rough estimates of necessary judge-time. These preliminary assessments permit the calendar attorney to assemble panels of cases in which common issues are decided by a single panel and the work-load is reasonably uniform among panels. Most important here, the groups of cases can then be matched with various panels of judges by a random process administered in the office of the clerk. There is no need for the Chief Judge to assign specific cases to specific judges, and thus this previously discussed element of concentrated judicial power is avoided. As a result, the additional dangers inherent in specialization can be partly offset when, as is true of some American courts, there is a central legal staff.

It is generally assumed that New Zealand judges are relatively reluctant to use cases as vehicles for law reform. Sir Kenneth Keith has cited Parliamentary sovereignty, the absence of a written constitution, and the relative ease of legislative reform as possible reasons.[30] The greater activism of American judges arguably accentuates the importance of policy understanding and, therefore,

[26] Constitution Act 1986, § 14 (1) (Parliament consists of sovereign in right of New Zealand and House of Representatives).

[27] US Const. art. I.

[28] Palmer, *supra*, ch. 4 n. 3, at 28–9.

[29] Telephone Conversation with Prof. Shelton, *supra*, ch. 3 n. 4.

[30] Keith, *supra*, ch. 4 n. 22, at 160. In recent years, however, greater activism has emerged. See, e.g., Cooke, *supra*, ch. 4 n. 22.

the benefits of judicial specialization. At the same time, however, those who object to judicial activism might resist specialization out of a belief that it would encourage further activism.

Finally, the American federal court system comprises a network of district courts and courts of appeals, each with responsibility for a defined geographic area, and each with the power to create its own precedents. In New Zealand, there is only one High Court (though it sits in various cities) and only one Court of Appeal.[31] Inter-court consistency is therefore more difficult to attain in the United States than it is in New Zealand. Since improved consistency is one of the principle objectives of specialized adjudication,[32] the extra difficulties of attaining consistency in the United States constitute an additional argument for specialization.

The governmental differences discussed up to this point relate broadly to separation of powers within the central government. Federalism principles also affect the desirability of judicial specialization. In a unitary system like that of New Zealand,[33] judges who sit on courts of general jurisdiction must contend with an especially broad array of legal questions. Issues like local planning law, valuation of land, and common law subjects such as contracts, property, and torts must be handled by the same judges who decide cases that raise what in the United States would be regarded as federal issues. As a result, legal generalism poses particular challenges for New Zealand High Court judges. In such a setting, the case for judicial specialization is arguably stronger.

New Zealand is part of the British Commonwealth,[34] but it is not clear which way that factor cuts. Its principal relevance here is that New Zealand judges are much more likely than American judges to elicit guidance from British cases. The British cases, in turn, generally reflect greater deference to the executive than do the American cases.[35] When the standard of review narrows, the

[31] See text accompanying *supra*, ch. 4 nn. 9–13. But see the Law Commission's proposal to replace the Court of Appeal with a 'Supreme Court' that would serve as New Zealand's court of final appeal. The Structure of the Courts, *supra*, ch. 4 n. 6, at xiii, Rec. No. 7.

[32] See text accompanying *supra*, ch. 1 nn. 23–7.

[33] Though New Zealand does not have states, it does have a highly developed system of local government. Palmer, *supra*, ch. 4 n. 3, at 5.

[34] Commonwealth Countries Act 1977, First Schedule.

[35] See, e.g., Davis, *supra*, ch. 1 n. 4, §§ 2. 17, 2. 18; Jaffe, *supra*, ch. 4 n. 147, at 2 (1969); M. Zander, *The Law-Making Process*, 230 (1980).

need for expertise diminishes and the benefits of specialization are lessened accordingly.[36] Again, however, those who would prefer a more active judicial role might welcome specialization as a device for encouraging it.

There are additional differences peculiar to the field of administrative justice. New Zealand has an Ombudsman's Office to investigate complaints against administrative bodies.[37] Arguably, this safeguard against ill-considered action reduces the need for knowledgeable experts at the adjudication stage. But in two other respects New Zealand judges might find special knowledge of administrative law more helpful than would American judges. The Administrative Procedure Act in the United States simplifies enormously the law that governs judicial review of administrative action.[38] New Zealand has not enacted similar legislation;[39] the introduction of the application for review, though simplifying the law somewhat, does not affect the technical limitations on the available judicial remedies.[40] The degree of technicality has been shown to be a significant factor influencing the desirability of specialized adjudication.[41] Moreover, unlike New Zealand, where full appeals from administrative tribunals to courts on questions of fact, law, and discretion are common,[42] such appeals are rare in the United States.[43] A broader judicial role favours a specialized adjudicative unit familiar with the underlying substantive policies.[44] These considerations provide greater reason to employ judicial specialization in administrative law in New Zealand than in the United States. (As discussed below, however, they seem offset by volume considerations that stem from geographic and demographic distinctions.)

[36] See *supra*, ch. 1 nn. 8–22 and accompanying text.

[37] See generally Ombudsman Act 1975. [38] 5 USC § 706.

[39] A New Zealand Administrative Procedure Act was proposed by Professor G. S. Orr, *supra*, Intro., n. 3, para. 318, but has not been enacted.

[40] See Judicature Amendment Act 1972, § 4, as amended by Judicature Amendment Act 1977, § 13.

[41] See *supra*, ch. 2, § B. 2.

[42] See *supra*, ch. 4 nn. 20–2 and accompanying text.

[43] The Administrative Procedure Act generally prescribes the 'substantial evidence' test and the 'arbitrary, capricious, or an abuse of discretion' test for review of factual and discretionary decisions, respectively. 5 USC § 706 (2)(A, E). A *de novo* trial is rare. See, e.g. 8 USC § 1105a (a) (5) (citizenship claims asserted as defences to deportation).

[44] See *supra*, ch. 1 nn. 8–22 and accompanying text.

In general, then, the differences between the legal systems of the United States and New Zealand have mixed effects on the usefulness of specialized adjudication systems. New Zealand judges must interpret a more rapidly changing set of laws that embrace both national and local issues. In administrative law they decide full appeals and apply some technical complexities in the law of judicial review. Further, the totality of the executive power, and the concentration of the remaining legislative power in a single chamber, increase the utility of knowledgeable specialists at the adjudicative level. In addition, New Zealand judges are far less likely than American judges to encounter broad constitutional issues that require the experience of legal generalists.

In competition with those factors are others that make judicial specialization more attractive in the United States than in New Zealand. American judges are more likely to invoke substantive policy when interpreting statutes, and in doing so they face more difficult problems of reconciliation with the decisions of courts that operate in other geographic areas. Moreover, power within the executive branch is more concentrated in the United States than it is in New Zealand, making knowledgeable specialists a more valuable check at the adjudication stage.

B. POPULATION, GEOGRAPHY, AND DEMOGRAPHICS

The differences based on the legal institutions and the systems of government might have mixed effects on the decision whether to specialize, but other differences point unequivocally in one direction. The most important of the relevant differences between New Zealand and the United States is sheer size. The United States has more than seventy times the population of New Zealand;[45] only one New Zealand city has more than 400,000 people.[46]

[45] As of the end of 1986, the New Zealand population was 3,307,084. Dept. of Statistics, *New Zealand Official Yearbook 1987–88*, Table 5.4 at 128 (92nd ann. edn., 1987). On 1 July 1986, the United States population was approximately 241,078,000. See Bureau of the Census, *Statistical Abstract of the United States*, 18 (108th edn., 1988).

[46] As of the end of 1986 the Auckland population was 820,754. Wellington, the next largest city, had only 325,697. Christchurch was third with 299,373. After that, the drop is sudden: Dunedin 106,864; Hamilton 101,814; Palmerston North 67,405. See *New Zealand Yearbook*, *supra*, n. 45, Table 5.6 at 131.

The huge United States population reinforces the case for specialization. The most obvious effect is on the volume of cases. As discussed earlier, the extremely small case-load of New Zealand's Administrative Division is probably the leading explanation for its disappointing reception. The higher volumes of American cases make it easier for specialized adjudicators to keep busy, and easier for them to realize the goals of expertise, efficiency, and consistency. In addition, the law of large numbers makes it more feasible to predict, and therefore to accommodate, fluctuations in the distribution of cases by subject-matter. Combined with the much larger land area of the United States,[47] the higher volume of total cases also results in the creation of more courts, and therefore greater difficulty in attaining nationwide uniformity. On this problem, specialization can help.[48] Moreover, the greater numbers of people and cases diminish the danger that the specialized community will become too clannish.[49]

Perhaps even more significant, the population density of the United States is more than twice that of New Zealand.[50] The two principal islands of New Zealand stretch a total of about 1,000 miles,[51] and the three main population centres are separated by significant distances.[52]

Given practical limits to the size of the geographic area that a single judicial district can effectively cover, one effect of a sparse and dispersed population is a small population per judicial district. With all else equal—including the propensity to litigate and the

[47] The land area of the United States is 3,539,289 sq. mls. *Statistical Abstract, supra*, n. 45, at 184. The area of New Zealand is 103,833 sq. mls. 20 *Encyclopedia Americana* at 245 (internat. edn., 1985). The United States area is thus about 34 times that of New Zealand.

[48] See *supra*, ch. 1 nn. 23–7 and accompanying text.

[49] See *supra*, ch. 2, § B. 7.

[50] As of the end of 1986, New Zealand had 3,307,084 people spread out among its 103,883 sq. mls., see *supra*, nn. 45, 47, a density of 31.8 people per sq. m. On 1 July 1986 the United States density was 68.1 per sq. m. See *Statistical Abstract, supra*, n. 45, at 19.

[51] See M. Lambert, E. Lambert, R. Palenski, K. Palenski (eds.), *Fourth Air New Zealand Almanac*, 174 (1986) (length exceeds 1,600 km.). At its widest point, New Zealand is 450 km. across. Ibid.

[52] From Auckland, in the northern part of the North Island, to Wellington, located at the southern tip of the North Island, is 660 km. Automobile Association, *Road Atlas of New Zealand*, 56 (1974). The distance from Picton (the ferry crossing point at the northern end of the South Island) to Christchurch, also on the South Island, is another 340 km. Ibid. at 77.

complexity of the cases filed[53]—a low nationwide population density therefore produces a small case-load per judicial district.

That fact is important because a large case-load per district renders operative, at the local level, many of the advantages of specialization that a large total population brings at the national level. When the case-load of a single adjudicative unit is large, the likelihood that specialization will foster both expertise and efficiency is enhanced. The same is true of consistency. A large case-load aggravates the difficulty of monitoring all the court's precedents and maintaining a reasonable degree of intra-court, intra-subject, consistency. And that is a problem that judicial concentration in a specialized field can help to minimize. Further, to the extent that a large case-load elevates the specialist adjudicators' degree of familiarity with the subject-matter, their capacity to identify, and conform to, the law of other districts is also strengthened. Similarly, a thriving case-load softens the efficiency problems associated with specialization by assuring that specialists will not be idle and by smoothing out fluctuations in the number of cases filed over time.

A large case-load per judicial district fortifies the argument for specialization in another way as well. One of the dangers of specialized adjudication, discussed earlier,[54] is the concentration of power in a small group of people. When a class of cases is large enough to command many judges, the disproportionate impact of the views of any one individual judge is lessened. Even in a large court, that sort of dispersal might be unrealistic when the specialized subject-matter is narrowly defined. But if the arguments put forward earlier for increased use of multiple-speciality adjudication systems are accepted,[55] then a court with a large case-load could quite feasibly assign the combined specialities to a significant number of its members.

[53] The combination of federal and state court systems in the United States, together with differences in the types of cases that New Zealand and the United States divert to administrative tribunals, make it difficult to compare propensity to litigate.

[54] See *supra*, paragraph of text following ch. 4 n. 182; see also *supra*, ch. 4 nn. 192–5 and accompanying text.

[55] See *supra*, ch. 3, § B.

Conclusion

The tide of specialization that has overtaken almost all professional disciplines has not left the legal profession unscathed. Lawyers specialize more frequently, and in subject-matter more narrowly defined, than ever before. Today, the same factors that have spurred both legal practitioners and academic lawyers to specialize are increasingly applicable to those responsible for adjudicating disputes. Adjudication by specialists has long been a central feature of adminstrative justice, but now it is rapidly spreading to the ordinary courts as well. The phenomenon is world-wide.

Before we go too far, it is crucial to isolate the question of specialization and to think carefully about its role in adjudication. In the first chapter, I have tried to set out with a reasonable degree of objectivity the advantages and disadvantages of specialization in achieving quality, efficiency, and public acceptance.

But cataloguing the costs and benefits, though essential, is not sufficient. A general theory capable of practical application also requires criteria by which one can identify those groups of cases in which the benefits of specialized adjudication would justify the costs. Chapter 2 attempts that task and suggests twelve such criteria to be consulted in the evaluation of future proposals for particular specialized bodies. Chapter 3, drawing on the first two chapters, then examines the possible models of specialized adjudication. I conclude there that the trend has actually been toward an intermediate degree of specialization, principally through the use of multiple-speciality adjudicators. I also believe this trend is a healthy one that should be affirmatively encouraged.

The Administrative Division of the New Zealand High Court is a useful vehicle both for testing and for illustrating the general theory of the first three chapters. As a case-study, it explores the potential strengths and weaknesses of specialized adjudication. The Division has produced some tangible but minor benefits, and no real costs thus far, other than any costs inherent in permitting appeals from administrative bodies to the High Court at all. The most serious obstacle to more substantial achievement is the lack of a case-load hefty enough to trigger the full benefits of specialization. In my view, the structure of the Division should in any event be altered to eliminate unnecessary and potentially dangerous concentrations of power.

Finally, any comparative study of specialized justice requires consideration of such inter-nation variables as the nations' systems of government, the characteristics of their legal institutions, and their demographies. The last chapter specifically contrasts New Zealand and the United States, but the variables it discusses are universal. As seen in that chapter, distinctions between Presidential and Parliamentary systems cut both ways, while factors like large population and high density favour specialized justice.

Appendix

First Report of the Public and Administrative Law Reform Committee of New Zealand
Appeals from Administrative Tribunals
(1968)

INTRODUCTION AND GENERAL

Public and Administrative Law Reform Committee

1. In July 1966 the Minister of Justice set up the Public and Administration Law Reform Committee under the chairmanship of Dr J. L. Robson, the Secretary for Justice. The members of the Committee are Professor C. C. Aikman, Dean of the Faculty of Law at the Victoria University of Wellington; Mr A. C. Brassington, a barrister and solicitor of Christchurch; Mr R. B. Cooke, one of Her Majesty's Counsel; Mr E. L. Greensmith C.M.G., a former Secretary to the Treasury; Dr R. G. McElroy, a barrister and solicitor and Mayor of Auckland; Professor J. F. Northey, Dean of the Faculty of Law at the University of Auckland; Mr G. S. Orr, Senior Crown Counsel; and Mr D. A. S. Ward, C.M.G., Counsel to the Law Drafting Office. The Secretary of the committee is Mr C. W. Ogilvie, Advisory Officer of the Department of Justice.

2. The matters for our investigation under a programme approved by the Law Revision Commission included appeals from administrative tribunals, the constitution and procedure of such tribunals and the judicial control of administrative acts. After some preliminary consideration it became clear that the last of these matters is less urgently in need of review than the others. Accordingly discussions and recommendations about certain administrative tribunals and rights of appeal form the main subject of this first report.

Administrative Tribunals in New Zealand

3. In New Zealand as in other developed countries the vast increase in the activities of government, both central and local, in the twentieth century has inevitably given rise to new categories of disputes or to a much greater number of disputes in categories already familiar. Some of

these disputes are between individual citizens on the one hand and the state or a local authority on the other. Some, while basically originating from State regulation of certain areas of economic or social activity, are between individual citizens on both sides or are occasioned immediately by clashes of interest between different sections of the community. In all of them, the public interest or the well-being of the community as a whole is involved. It is natural to assume, in a democratic country accustomed to the rule of law, that so far as reasonably practicable these disputes should be settled by adjudication. That is to say, by common consent what is called for is a process which will enable the facts to be ascertained; the differing points of view or arguments to be effectively presented; all the relevant points to be weighed with manifest care; and an impartial and informed decision to be made. Perhaps this can be summed up more simply as the need for a fair hearing.

4. To illustrate those somewhat abstract propositions by concrete examples, we mention a few of the disputes that come before some of the main tribunals considered later in our report. To carry out their increased functions government departments and other public bodies must acquire land; it is recognized that fair compensation should be paid to individuals whose property is taken; and disputes as to the amount go before local Land Valuation Committees. From their decisions there is a right of appeal to the Land Valuation Court, which is at present the final arbiter in New Zealand between the citizen and the State in this major field. Again, control of the use of land is essential for the economic and social welfare of the community—hence the existence of town and country planning and the Town and Country Planning Appeal Boards. These boards determine appeals from decisions of local authorities or their planning committees. Such disputes may be between citizens objecting to a proposed use of land by fellow citizens or between a local authority, formulating a restrictive plan, and citizens whose properties will be affected thereby. As a last example, economic and social experience has led to the regulation of the transport industry by a licensing system; disputes about the grant and the scope of licences are ultimately determined by the Transport Licensing Appeal Authority, but the bulk of the work is disposed of at first instance by the various District Licensing Authorities.

5. As those examples indicate, the disputes accompanying the modern surge of governmental activity are often of great importance to the persons immediately concerned and to the general public. As a broad group these disputes may be said without exaggeration to affect the lives of more people than most of the issues dealt with at present by the older-established courts. These courts—'the ordinary courts', as they are often

conveniently called by lawyers and others—exist for the very purpose of adjudication. They are manned by judges and magistrates whose experience, capacity and training are likely to make them better equipped than other persons to carry out the responsible and exacting work of determining disputes. Yet, as the examples we have mentioned also indicate, these courts have often not been chosen by the legislature to determine disputes produced by the control of present-day society. Jurisdiction has been vested instead in a diverse collection of specialised courts or tribunals which for convenience can broadly be described as administrative tribunals. We think it necessary to examine the reasons for this.

6. There are several reasons for the creation of administrative tribunals as adjudicatory bodies in addition to the ordinary courts. In considering these it is as well to bear in mind the differences between jurisdiction at first instance and appellate jurisdiction. At first instance the volume of administrative adjudication and the relative unimportance of a good deal of it would make the use of the ordinary courts impractical. Obviously the ordinary courts could not cope, unless transformed, with every land valuation, town and country planning or transport licensing dispute in New Zealand or with the multifarious other disputes that come for their first (and usually final) hearing before administrative tribunals of one kind or another. Nor is there any need to suggest such a transformation. Most disputes are solved at first instance, more or less to the satisfaction of the parties and relatively cheaply and expeditiously. Apart from the volume of work, other factors which have justifiably played some part in the creation of administrative tribunals of first instance are the need for relative informality; the avoidance of unnecessary expense; and on occasions a desire for special qualifications in at any rate some members of the tribunal.

7. Not all the points just mentioned apply to all administrative tribunals. Nevertheless, as stated in the United Kingdom by the Committee on Administrative Tribunals and Enquiries (the Franks Committee):

> Reflection on the general social and economic changes of recent decades convinces us that tribunals as a system for adjudication have come to stay. The tendency for issues arising from legislative schemes to be referred to special tribunals is likely to grow rather than to diminish.[1]

8. We accept that administrative tribunals are a valuable, and indeed an essential, part of the constitutional machinery of a modern democratic state such as New Zealand. Our attention has therefore been directed

[1] Report of the Committee on Administrative Tribunals and Enquiries Cmnd. 218 (1957) para. 37.

towards improvements in the present system. Although some of our recommendations relate to the first instance level, it is at the appellate level that we believe improvements can chiefly be made at this stage.

9. As to the appellate level, the reasons that can be advanced for not making use of the ordinary courts, and the Supreme Court in particular, are in our opinion either unconvincing or capable of being met by the changes we recommend. The nature of the appellate work demands legal qualifications, as has been recognized by Parliament in requiring that various appellate tribunals which have been set up should either consist of or be presided over by barristers or solicitors of (usually) seven years practice or standing. This is similar in terms to the qualification laid down for appointment to the Supreme Court, but there has been a tendency to set up a special tribunal rather than to make use of the Supreme Court.

10. One reason for this is probably that the different jurisdictions have been constituted by statute at different times, as a need has been felt, without any integrated plan and often without regard to the wider constitutional implications of the particular statute. Thus to take a few leading illustrations, the Land Valuation Court was created in 1948; the Town and Planning Appeal Board was created in 1953, though its origin may be traced to 1926; the Transport Licensing Appeal Authority was created in 1949, though a somewhat similar appeal authority had been constituted in 1941 and there had been provision for Appeal Boards previously, going as far back as 1931; the Trade Practices Appeal Authority was created in 1958; and the Price Tribunal was created in 1947, though in large measure replacing a jurisdiction established under emergency regulations during the second world war. Administrative tribunals, even at appellate level, are no new thing; but only comparatively recently have they attracted any marked attention, as the growth in their numbers and the importance of their work have come to be appreciated.

11. The fact that the Supreme Court has not in the past played as full a part in this field as we think it should play in the future has been contributed to by the attitude of the legal profession itself. At times there has been a lack of interest in the comparatively new subject of administrative law and a reluctance on the part of judges to become involved in its problems. The former Solicitor-General, Mr H. R. C. Wild Q.C., who advocated increased use of the courts in administrative matters, has himself conceded that the profession's own attitude has contributed to the increasing reliance on administrative tribunals.:[2]

> . . . the organised profession has shown too little readiness to tackle the problem of adapting legal institutions to modern requirements . . . The

[2] See 'Social Progress and the Legal Process', 27 N.Z.J.P.A., March 1965, § (1).

view that detachment from politics should not be prejudiced by requiring a decision on what is a question of policy and not a justiciable issue is one thing, but unwillingness on the part of a judge to use his resourcefulness in applying a new piece of social legislation is quite another. The insistence of some judges on the letter rather than the object of legislation has encouraged the tribunal system just as in the past, in New Zealand, reluctance that the Supreme Court should be given new jurisdictions led to the establishment of special courts.

12. We believe that the attitude referred to is by no means generally prevalent today, either on the Supreme Court bench or in the legal profession. It is true, however, that a degree of specialisation and consistency of approach is important in the determination of *appeals* from *administrative tribunals*. This would be more difficult to attain if a case might come before any one of the Supreme Court judges. One of our purposes in recommending, as we do in this report, the establishment of an Administrative Division of the Supreme Court is to overcome that difficulty.

13. It appears to us that we should aim at preserving the advantages of an administrative tribunal system and eliminating its disadvantages as far as possible. The advantages we have already outlined. The main disadvantages are connected with the quality of the adjudication involved in such a system. The tribunals cannot always be comprised of persons especially well-equipped to adjudicate. In consequence the decision may be incorrect or—equally important—the parties may not be satisfied with the hearing they have received. We have come to the conclusion that the two-fold aim we have mentioned can best be achieved by (i) providing the best possible rights of appeal, and (ii) making certain improvements as regards the personnel and procedure of administrative tribunals at first instance.

Types of Tribunals

14. We have not yet considered tribunals regulating the entry into or expulsion from a profession or trade, or domestic tribunals such as those set up by sporting bodies. But apart from these there are over sixty administrative tribunals in New Zealand. Some of them meet but rarely, others are in almost constant session. Some deal in relatively unimportant matters, others have jurisdiction over matters as important either directly to the parties or to the community as a whole as almost anything that is dealt with by the Supreme Court.

15. Administrative tribunals can be classified in a number of ways, depending on what is to be emphasized. One classification referred to in

'The British Commonwealth: New Zealand' [3] edited by J. L. Robson is according to their distance from political control:

(i) Those tribunals which consist of public servants who by virtue of some statutory office are called upon to exercise their powers in a judicial manner. Examples are the Commissioner of Patents and the Registrar-General of Land.
(ii) The intermediate type of organ which lies outside the orthodox government department, having members recruited as a rule from outside the regular public service. There are many such instances, for example the Air Services Licensing Authority and the Crimes Compensation Tribunal.
(iii) Bodies designated as special courts. These are the Court of Arbitration, the Land Valuation Court, the Compensation Court and the Maori Land Court.

Tribunals can also be classified according to their function. Some have power to make legislative orders, that is, orders in general terms which govern the action of classes of persons. Some conduct hearings and make orders or decisions which affect only the parties concerned. Some exercise executive or administrative functions where policy considerations predominate. Some tribunals, for example the Price Tribunal, exercise all these functions at different times.

16. A further alternative classification is according to subject matter:

> Tribunals concerned with licensing (e.g. cinematograph films, transport, liquor, milk), tribunals concerned with trade (e.g. restrictive trade practices, prices), tribunals concerned with health and social security (e.g. medical advertisements, invalid benefits), those concerned with land (e.g. land settlement, land valuation, town and country planning), those concerned with local government and those concerned with State Services employees.

17. Whatever classification is used, administrative tribunals in New Zealand show a rich variety. In undertaking the investigation our dominant purpose has been to find the structure and arrangement which will achieve the best decisions in the particular field of each tribunal. Subject to that, we have attempted to discover whether in respect of this variety of consistent, coherent pattern of constitution, procedure, appeal rights and so on, could be achieved.

18. As Mr G. S. Orr has pointed out, no very rational principles underlie the formation and composition of many administrative tribunals. Their structure and powers largely depend on the particular inclinations of the

[3] Published by Stevens: First edition p. 103.

Minister responsible at the time, and there may or may not be a right of appeal in part or in whole.[4] This right of appeal lies in some cases to the ordinary courts but in most cases it is to a further administrative body, the ordinary courts exercising control only on jurisdictional issues or where an error of law appears on the face of the record. 'The Citizen and Power', published by the Department of Justice in 1965, lists the tribunals from which a right of appeal exists, and to what body the appeal lies.

Criticisms of Existing System

19. Features of the existing system have been criticized. A special committee set up by the New Zealand Law Society to consider appeals from administrative tribunals said:

> We think there is little doubt that the chief cause of dissatisfaction with the prevailing system, if such it can be called, of administrative justice is the inability to have decisions of tribunals on questions of fact, or the exercise of their statutory discretions, reviewed in the ordinary courts. In a measure, we suspect, this sort of dissatisfaction is superficial, in that it can be not much more than a mask for dissatisfaction with the policy or principles of the legislation administered by the tribunal. But, over and above this, we believe that there is quite a deep-rooted feeling in the community that justice administered by bodies other than the ordinary courts tends, from the point of view of fairness and care, to be an inferior brand of justice. We do not think this view wholly without foundation, although we recognise that at times administrative tribunals attain a high standard and we are far from making any universal criticism of them.

20. The Law Society committee recommended that provisions be enacted for conferring rights of appeal on questions of law to the courts of law from all statutory tribunals, with certain very limited exceptions of which the most important is the Court of Arbitration. Indeed, they went further and recommended that decisions of statutory tribunals on issues of importance should be subject to appeal to the ordinary courts on questions of fact or discretion except where there are special reasons to the contrary.

21. In a paper delivered to the Commonwealth Law Conference in Sydney in 1965, the then Solicitor-General of New Zealand, Mr Wild, took much the same view. He considered that all tribunal decisions should be reviewable in the courts on points of law, and where appropriate on the merits also. He said—

[4] 'Report on Administrative Justice in New Zealand' (1964).

> This is not merely a question of the dignity and status of the courts. It is a question whether the really important decisions affecting the citizen are being made by the men best qualified by training and experience to make them; whether the community is losing the benefit of the influence of the courts in moulding the law in action.

He said further—

> . . . there should always be a right of general appeal except where the tribunal's jurisdiction is very limited in value or where an expert body is dealing with a non-justiciable issue. In particular, it is the choice of the appeal authority that needs review. In some measure this must depend on the subject matter, and in some cases an appellate tribunal will be appropriate. But where, as at present in the important areas of trade practices and road and air transport licensing in New Zealand, it is thought right to give an appeal from a non-expert tribunal to an authority with legal qualifications, it is better that the appeal should go to a court.

22. These then are some of the criticisms of the present system. It must be pointed out however that there are other persons, for whose opinion respect is due, who consider that the present system works reasonably satisfactorily and are doubtful of the wisdom of giving any increased jurisdiction to the courts. They would nevertheless agree that the present system could be improved in certain ways.

23. His Honour Judge Archer, who has had considerable experience with a number of tribunals, said in a paper to the Australia and New Zealand Association of Law Students Conference in Wellington in May 1967:

> What is wrong, in so far as anything is wrong, is with the particular tribunals which make up the system, with the statutory provisions constituting these tribunals, and with the persons serving on tribunals. There are no doubt tribunals with powers too wide to be generally acceptable, and tribunals set up for purposes for which an administrative tribunal is not a suitable instrument. These are matters for which the Legislature is responsible and which the Legislature could readily correct. It is said we have too many administrative tribunals, but surely the only sound test of this is whether any of them can with advantage be dispensed with.

24. Judge Archer argued in the paper against any suggestion that a right of appeal from the present appeal tribunals to the ordinary courts should be given on fact and discretion. Nevertheless he favours appointment of

the judges of the Arbitration and Compensation Courts to the Supreme Court bench and, to that extent, a measure of integration.

25. The Committee obtained the views of the permanent heads of those departments which were involved with administrative tribunals. Their general opinion was that the present arrangements were largely satisfactory.

The Committee's Approach

26. No-one would deny that, whether or not any particular criticism can be justified and whether or not any particular tribunal can be said to be working reasonable satisfactorily, there is a need to review the working of the administrative tribunal system just as there is need to review other aspects of our law. The Minister of Justice in 'The Law in a Changing Society' stated:

> The purpose of the law is to do justice and to secure the order of society. To achieve these things it provides rules and standards governing some of the multifarious relationships of men with one another and of men with the organised community which we know as the State. As these relationships increase, develop and alter, so must the law. The complex nature of advanced societies calls for a complex law, and a changing society requires a law that will respond to changing needs and demands. To the extent that ways of thought and life alter, the law must change if it is to be in touch with life, work justice and command respect.

27. This of course applies to administrative law, and to administrative tribunals, no less than to other branches of the law. We have therefore the opportunity—and indeed the duty—to assess the adequacy of the present system in the light of first principles. As far as we are aware no Government-appointed body in New Zealand has before been given the task of thoroughly and systematically investigating the administrative tribunals of this country. We consider that our responsibility is to recommend more than makeshift or piecemeal reforms, and that we are expected to suggest a system which we regard as best ensuring that the needs and aspirations of today's citizens are met.

28. Although we have concentrated throughout on the need for a reassessment of the administrative tribunal system so as to keep up with the changing needs of society, we believe that the ordinary judicial system should likewise be reviewed from time to time in the light of current needs. Such a task is not within our terms of reference except in so far as it impinges on the problem of administrative law.

29. From the outset we were satisfied that it would be wrong to approach our terms of reference by trying to devise some ideal pattern for an administrative tribunal system and then trying to fit or force various tribunals into that pattern. Our method of working has been intended to be a more practical one. It has not been based on any preconceived idea. What we have done has been time-consuming but, we think, rewarding. We have examined in detail a number of tribunals of different types and functions and we have consulted various people closely associated with them. Apart from those consulted, some members of the Committee have had considerable experience of appearing before most of the tribunals studied and could therefore speak with first-hand knowledge. The tribunals so far studied are:

(1) The Land Valuation Court;
(2) The Town and Country Planning Appeal Board;
(3) { The Transport Licensing Authorities;
  The Transport Licensing Appeal Authority;
(4) The Transport Charges Appeal Authority;
(5) { The Trade Practices & Prices Commission;
  The Trade Practices Appeal Authority;
(6) The Price Tribunal.

30. Among those consulted in relation to these tribunals were: Judge K. G. Archer, Judge of the Land Valuation Court and former Transport Licensing Appeal Authority; Mr J. Bruce Brown, Valuer-General; Mr W. L. Ellingham, barrister and solicitor; Mr A. E. Hurley, barrister and solicitor; Mr J. W. Kealy S.M., Chairman of the Town and Country Planning Appeal Board; Mr P. L. Laing, Commissioner of Works; Mr J. H. Luxford S.M., Transport Licensing Appeal Authority; Mr R. J. McLachlan, Director-General of Land; Mr M. J. Moriarty, Secretary of Industries and Commerce; Mr M. J. O'Brien, barrister and solicitor; Mr R. J. Polaschek, Commissioner of Transport; Mr. W. G. Smith, barrister and solicitor; Mr P. C. M. Straubel, barrister and solicitor; Mr A. B. Thomson, City Solicitor, Wellington City Council; Mr J. W. P. Watts, Chairman of the Special Town and Country Planning Appeal Board.

We acknowledge our indebtedness to all those who kindly gave us the benefit of their experience in each particular field.

31 The result of our mode of approach has been interesting. As we have moved over the ground, passing from one tribunal to another and not infrequently retracing our steps to obtain a second or a third view, the varying and tentative views held by the members of the Committee at the beginning have gradually come closer together and at the same time

crystallised. A genuine and almost unanimous consensus has emerged. Our main recommendation, concurred in by all members of the Committee save one, is that an Administrative Division of the Supreme Court be established to hear Appeals from certain administrative tribunals. We are satisfied that this step would offer the best assurance that the very important issues arising in such appeals are decided justly. It would be the best means of satisfying the public that each case receives a fair and thorough hearing and a carefully-considered decision.

32. In reviewing the merits of the present system of administrative justice at the appellate level, the Committee considered a number of alternatives. One was the preservation of the status quo, a view which, as we have pointed out, is not without support, despite the criticisms levelled at it. The Committee considered, however, that many of the criticisms were justified. We now mention some of the unsatisfactory features of the present situation—

(i) Taking the broad view, there seems little justification for the inconsistency of the present arrangements. There is a bewildering variety of appeal rights (or lack of them), of types of appellate bodies, of constitutions, procedure and jurisdiction. The present complexity appears to have been unplanned, or possibly the result of different plans at different times. We think it would be difficult to argue that it is justifiable or that a more simple, rational system could not be devised without attempting to force particular jurisdictions into a theoretical straitjacket.

(ii) We have been impressed with the criticism made by one of our members, Mr G. S. Orr, of the constitution and status of the present appeal authorities. While no-one questions the ability of the persons holding office as the appeal authorities, it is clear that their status is not readily understood and this tends to create a wrong impression in parties to the proceedings. No matter what may be the quality of the decision, some of those involved think they have received less than justice.

(iii) It should be recognized that in order to give the administrative tribunal system the importance it deserves, New Zealand must provide more settled and attractive terms of appointment for those called on to decide questions in these fields. The Committee have noted the hand-to-mouth arrangements and haphazard appointments of appellate authorities. Appointment is made 'during pleasure' or at the most for a limited number of years. In the circumstances recruitment becomes difficult,and it is surprising that New Zealand has been as well served as it has been. Often the appointments have been held by the judges of the Land Valuation Court and of the

Compensation Court, since the work of these Courts did not wholly occupy the judges. Reallocation of appointments becomes necessary when the judge retires or dies or no longer has the time available.

33. The second alternative considered by the Committee was the giving of a general right of appeal from administrative tribunals to the Supreme Court analogous to the general right of appeal from Magistrates' Courts to the Supreme Court. This was considered to have certain disadvantages. Primarily the disadvantages centre on the questions of expertise and specialization. While the value of special knowledge and experience can be exaggerated in this context, we have no doubt that real advantages are to be gained by ensuring that administrative appeals are dealt with by a limited number of judges specializing *inter alia* in the field of administrative appeals. This would make for consistency of judicial policy and approach and for the ready acquisition of skill and experience in dealing with the problems of administrative law. It would also make for economy of effort.

34. A third alternative was the creation of an Administrative Court, separate from the Supreme Court but intended to have in its own field a status akin to that of the Supreme Court. The arguments for this alternative were fully put to us, during our deliberations, by Mr Orr and are stated by him in an appendix to this report. After careful consideration, however, we find ourselves unable to accept them. Our main reasons are as follows—

(i) Whether or not a new Administrative Court was deemed by statute to have the status of the present Supreme Court, many would inevitably regard it as inferior. Its status in fact would tend to be little higher than that of the present appeal authorities. There would be difficulty in attracting suitable persons to sit as judges of the Court. Members of the public involved as parties would continue to suspect, rightly or wrongly, that they had been accorded second-class justice. Appeals from administrative tribunals raise issues of first-class importance in modern society. So far as humanly possible, they should be dealt with, and manifestly be seen to be dealt with, by a court of appropriate stature both in fact and in theory.

(ii) In an attempt to meet the difficulties just mentioned, the suggestion has been made of appointing the judges of an Administrative Court as judges of the Supreme Court but entirely separating the two courts in theory and almost entirely separating the judges of the two courts in fact. This strikes us as a clumsy and rather transparent device, especially in New Zealand conditions. With a population of the size of ours we do not think there is room for more than one truly

Supreme Court in the commonly accepted sense. It cannot be right, we think to appoint to that court persons who are only nominal members of it. All the members should be Supreme Court judges in the fullest sense, although those assigned to the proposed Administrative Division would, among their other functions, specialise in the work of that Division.

(iii) The establishment of a separate Administrative Court would raise problems as to its relationship with the Supreme Court. If an attempt were made by statute to give it theoretically equal status, there would be a danger that the two courts would give conflicting and irreconcilable decisions. To endeavour to prevent this, unless yet a third court in the nature of a *tribunal de conflits* were brought into play, it would be necessary that one of the two courts should have the final word as to the respective jurisdictions of each. In the upshot the Administrative Court would be found, we think, to occupy a somewhat subordinate position; so that the difficulties of status to which we have already referred would not be removed. At present the Supreme Court has a supervisory jurisdiction over all other courts in New Zealand except the Court of Appeal. It might well be difficult to draft a provision which would totally oust that jurisdiction in respect of any new court.

(iv) Administrative law is far from being limited to appeals from administrative tribunals. There are for example the common law remedies of certiorari, prohibition and mandamus (often collectively called the prerogative writs) whereby the Supreme Court ensures that tribunals of limited jurisdiction and other public bodies act within their powers. Moreover many cases involving the interpretation of statutes may fairly be said to come within the field of administrative law. In general it is obviously desirable that all administrative law cases at a certain level should be dealt with by the same group of judges. For example, the court which hears the statutory appeals should also in general hear the prerogative writ applications. We are not prepared to recommend that the latter jurisdiction, which goes to the very root of our constitutional system and is a valued protection of the rights of citizens, should be taken away from the Supreme Court and vested in a new type of court.

Administrative Division of Supreme Court

35. Consideration of the various alternatives has led us, as already mentioned, to the firm conclusion that an Administrative Division of the Supreme Court is the logical and acceptable solution in New Zealand. We think that anything that might be achieved by a separate Administrat-

ive Court is more likely to be achieved by an Administrative Division. The Division would hear appeals from certain administrative tribunals, and we shall indicate hereinafter particular rights of appeal which we recommend. It would also exercise the present jurisdiction of the Supreme Court in administrative law. It would have the desirable attributes of status and specialization. This recommendation would meet the major criticism of the present system that the Excecutive has kept justiciable issues outside the jurisdiction of the ordinary courts. The conferment of the appellate jurisdiction on the Supreme Court (in the modified form we have indicated) would inspire greater public confidence, by reason of the higher status of the appellate body.

36. It is important to make clear what we regard as implicit in our recommendation of an Administrative Division.

(i) *Membership of Administrative Division* The judges of the Administrative Division of Supreme Court should be assigned by the Governor-General to the Division, and as Supreme Court judges they would also perform other Supreme Court work when required. Without making a hard-and-fast recommendation as to numbers, we suggest that at this stage a Division of three or four judges would be adequate.

(ii) *Qualifications of Judges* Persons appointed to the Administrative Division should have a full appreciation of the need to give effect to the economic and social policies the legislation was designed to implement. It is perhaps hardly necessary to add, but to avoid any possible misunderstandings we do so, that they should also possess the other qualities appropriate to Supreme Court judges.

(iii) *Lay Members* There should be no bar to the appointment of lay members or assessors to sit with the Court if and when desirable.

(iv) *Expense* The proceedings in the Administrative Division should not be more expensive than proceedings before the present appellate administrative tribunals.

(v) *Informality* The atmosphere should not be more formal than that of appellate administrative tribunals.

(vi) *Consistency* It is clearly desirable that there should be a degree of specialization among the judges so that the virtue of consistency is not lost. The judges would handle throughout New Zealand the matters assigned to the Division and would when necessary travel to appropriate hearing places. In cases of special importance we envisage that a full court (probably comprised of three judges) of the Administrative Division could sit.

37. In these ways we are aiming to retain the advantages of the present appellate structure while adding advantages which we deem crucial, namely, the greater consistency, coherence and authority an Administrative Division would bring. In our view the synthesis of these virtues is perfectly feasible and would fit New Zealand conditions ideally.

38. While it would not be possible for Supreme Court judges without special assignment to sit in the Division, we consider there are a number of judges who would be most suited to the task and who could be invited to accept membership of the Division. Thus recruitment could be either direct from the present bench or from the bar.

39. Our recommendation is not a radical one, inasmuch as it is essentially a proposal to adapt and improve existing institutions. This seems to be the way in which progress is usually made in English-speaking countries. Our proposal for some degree of specialization on the Supreme Court bench in one field is probably in conformity with a general tendency. As population and the total volume of work increase, it is no doubt inevitable that a certain amount of specialization will take place among the judges. The reconstitution of the court of Appeal in 1957 may be regarded as one manifestation of this tendency. Irrespective of our recommendations, we think it is likely to continue.

40. Where an appeal on a point of law from the Administrative Division is appropriate it would lie to the Court of Appeal. This would add to the public confidence which we expect to follow from the setting up of the Administrative Division. As a natural and single step the highest New Zealand court would become the ultimate appeal body in New Zealand where important legal questions are involved, just as it is now in regard to cases which are heard by the courts in the ordinary way.

Meaning of 'Point of Law'

41. The application of the phrase 'point of law' or 'question of law' is not always clear. As Professor Northey pointed out in a paper prepared for the Committee, in various contexts errors of law could fall under one or more of the following heads—

(1) Excess or want of jurisdiction;
(2) Error of law on the face of the record;
(3) Misconstruction of a statute, regulation or document;
(4) Non-compliance with the relevant legislative provisions;

(5) Some errors concerning evidence;
(6) Determinations based on irrelevant considerations or so unreasonable as to amount to a failure to exercise the power of decision;
(7) Some instances of refusal to exercise jurisdiction;
(8) Breach of the principles of natural justice.

Professor Northey suggests that in providing for an appeal on law Parliament should reduce the uncertainty by enacting an inclusive definition. We wish to give further consideration to whether or not such a definition is practicable or desirable. As the question does not affect the substance of our general recommendations it need not be discussed at this stage.

Membership of Tribunals

42. In addition to the basic recommendation for the establishment of an Administrative Division of the Supreme Court, we recommend certain changes in relation to particular tribunals of first instance and to particular appellate tribunals which, in our view, should not be absorbed into the Administrative Division. As the Franks Committee has stated, the general standard of adjudication of administrative tribunals depends on the degree of competence of members of the tribunal. We recognize that in New Zealand the reputation and public acceptability of a particular administrative tribunal has often depended much on the calibre of its members. There are general principles which should be observed as to the qualifications of members of these tribunals, and as to the method of their appointment—

(i) The chairmen of all appellate tribunals should be legally qualified.
(ii) In general it is desirable that the chairman of a tribunal of first instance—including a single member where the tribunal consists of a single member—should be legally qualified. This, however, may not always be possible or appropriate. In that event he should at least be disinterested and possessed of qualifications and experience that equip him for membership of the tribunal concerned, having regard to its status and functions.
(iii) Any other members of appellate tribunals and tribunals of first instance should also be disinterested and possess qualifications and experience equipping them for membership of the tribunal concerned, having regard to its status and functions.
(iv) In principle, particular interests ought not to be specifically represented on administrative tribunals.
(v) Appointments to administrative tribunals should be made by the Governor-General acting on the advice of the Minister concerned.

The Minister should, however, be required to consult the Minister of Justice before tendering his advice. We regard this point as particularly important. As well as helping to ensure that the appointee is suitable, it should dispel any illusion that the department of state administering the tribunal may be exercising undue control over its personnel.

(vi) Members of administrative tribunals should be appointed for a term of not less than three years and there should be standard grounds for removal.

MINORITY VIEW

An Administrative Court

1. While being whole-heartedly in favour of a rationalization of the present system I consider the setting up of an Administrative Division of the Supreme Court to be unwise. Such a Division will inevitably take on the colour of the Supreme Court substantially as it now exists. Yet the widely acknowledged unsuitability of courts such as the Supreme Court as an appellate body from adminstrative tribunals has been the main reason over the years for setting up special courts and other appellate authorities both here and throughout the Commonwealth.

2. The proposal of the majority involves the rejection of this widespread experience and practice. Clearly reasons of the most compelling kind are needed by way of justification. In my view they do not exist. The proposal constitutes a radical innovation in preference to the more pragmatic solution involved in setting up an Administrative Court. Such a court would be essentially a consolidation of the present appellate bodies in one body in a way which retains their many advantages and at the same time eliminates their defects.

3. Among the reasons for my apprehension of the majority's proposal are the following:

(a) *Over-Judicialization* The establishment of an Administrative Division would lead to over-judicialization of the various matters at present deliberately excluded from the Supreme Court's jurisdiction. Thus, proceedings would tend to be assimilated more closely to the adversary system which is not always suited to the adjudication of matters of social and economic policy. Procedures and evidentiary rules would tend to be stricter and relevant statutes less likely to be adequately construed and applied.

(b) *Less Constructive Decisions* Judges of the Supreme Court would understandably be less inclined to make decisions which on occasions are necessarily controversial. Instead they would tend to adopt a more passive role in keeping with the tradition of the Supreme Court rather than implement social economic or industrial policy in a constructive way.

(c) *Loss of Impartiality of the Supreme Court* With relatively few exceptions all the powers likely to be vested in the Administrative Division would involve value judgments on matters of social and economic policy. This is at variance with the traditional and invaluable role of the Supreme Court of disinterestedness and impartiality which should be preserved unimpaired.

(d) *Loss in Informality* There would be a marked loss in informality and freedom of access to the court and a likely increase in costs to litigants, more of whom would feel obliged to instruct counsel or not appear at all.

(e) *Less Specialization* There is less likelihood of specialization in particular areas and of the development of consistency in approach.

(f) *Loss of Flexibility* The proposal for an Administrative Division is made after an examination of some only of the existing appellate bodies. The committee has yet to consider how suitable the proposed Division will be for the remaining jurisdictions. Its relative inflexibility limits its usefulness in the wide field of administrative justice.

4 I believe the cumulative weight of the foregoing defects to be such as seriously to raise the question whether, on balance, any significant improvement will be achieved. In any event, these deficiencies can, I believe, be avoided if appellate jurisdiction is vested in an Administrative Court. Such a Court would exercise general appellate jurisdiction over administrative tribunals. The new Court would absorb the Land Valuation Court, the Compensation Court and preferably, the Court of Arbitration. The proposal does not involve a proliferation of courts but rather a reduction. No more judges would be needed than will be required for the same work in an Administrative Division of the Supreme Court. The Administrative Court could sit in a number of Divisions dealing respectively with Licensing in all forms; Industrial affairs; Trade Practices and Prices and Local Government which would include Town Planning and Land Valuation. In important cases the judges of the Court could, where desirable, sit as a full court. There would be a right of appeal

on all questions of law to the Court of Appeal. These proposals are spelt out in more detail in my Report on Administrative Justice in New Zealand[1] and have been amplified in the 1965 K. J. Scott Memorial Lecture[2] and ANZALS address.[3]

5. The principal objection of the majority to a separate Administrative Court appears to be that, in its view, such a Court would inevitably be regarded as inferior in status to the Supreme Court. This is very questionable. A single unified court embracing the broad field of administrative justice would readily stand alongside the Supreme Court. The only danger is that it might conceivably overshadow the Supreme Court as some protagonists for enlarging the jurisdiction of the Supreme Court clearly fear. The suggestion of the majority that the status of the Administrative Court would in fact tend to be little better than the present appeal authorities appears to be based on a misconception of the role that such a court would play in the economic, social and industrial affairs of the community. The objection of the majority loses any substance it may have if judges of the Administrative Court are also appointed judges of the Supreme Court. They could, as opportunity arose, assist in certain work of the Supreme Court although the work of the Administrative Court would naturally engross the greater part of their time just as judges appointed to an Administrative Division would be occupied mainly on the work of that Division.

6. Two lesser matters are advanced by the majority as reasons why they cannot recommend the establishment of an Administrative Court. One is an alleged danger that the new court would create parallel but conflicting systems of jurisprudence and, in particular, the possibility is envisaged that the two independent courts would give conflicting and irreconcilable decisions. This criticism entirely overlooks that the two courts would on all questions of law be subject to the same higher court, the New Zealand Court of Appeal. Any conflicting decisions would be reconciled on appeal in the same way that conflicting decisions among judges of the Supreme Court are at present reconciled and in precisely the same way that conflicting decisions between judges of the proposed Administrative Division and other judges of the Supreme Court would be reconciled. The other objection relates only to a matter of drafting. It is suggested that it would be difficult to draft a provision which would oust the Supreme Court's supervisory jurisdiction over the Administrative Court. These difficulties are not spelt out. I am confident that the Law Draftsman would not find it a difficult task to draft the single short clause needed to

1. Government Printer 1964.
2. New Zealand Journal of Public Administration March 1966.
3. Unpublished.

achieve the desirable objective of keeping each Court within its own sphere of jurisdiction.

7. The obvious necessity of preventing the Supreme Court from being involved in controversy over current social, economic and industrial matters inherent in administrative appellate work necessarily imposes limits on both the kind of work which can properly be assigned to it and, as already suggested, the effectiveness with which such work can be performed. The vesting of appellate functions in an Administrative Court would insulate the Supreme Court from the critical comment which decisions in this more controversial area inevitably attract from time to time. So far the Committee has considered a limited number only of appellate bodies. Among those yet to be considered is the Court of Arbitration. No one would question the national importance of the work of this Court. It is difficult to conceive of its being absorbed into an Administrative Division of the Supreme Court. The pungent criticisms which its periodic controversial decisions attract should not be directed at the Supreme Court. In any event its basic function is one of arbitration rather than adjudication in the traditional manner of the Supreme Court. Yet there are obvious advantages in merging the Arbitration Court into one unified court concerned with the wide range of social, economic and industrial matters. This would terminate the present isolation of the Judge of this court from his judicial colleagues, and would allow some desirable diversification of work. I am unaware of any significant impediments to the absorption of this court into the proposed Administrative Court and the advantages are readily apparent. As with other Judges of this court the Judge exercising the jurisdiction of the former Court of Arbitration could also be a Judge of the Supreme Court. In this way, appropriate status would be secured while at the same time criticism of industrial and economic decisions would be directed at the Administrative Court and not the Supreme Court which should be kept clear of the battle. In the same way the jurisdiction of the various Government Service Tribunals such as the Public Service, Post Office and Railways Tribunals could readily be vested in the Administrative Court. Here again these have not yet been considered by the Committee. They would fit very uneasily indeed in an Administrative Division of the Supreme Court.

8. Quite apart from the Court of Arbitration the proposed Administrative Court could readily absorb the jurisdiction of the Price Tribunal which the majority would re-name the Price Appeal Tribunal and otherwise leave intact. The majority recognize that the work of this Tribunal should not be vested in an Administrative Division of the Supreme Court. Yet this Tribunal is from time to time called upon to make decisions involving millions of dollars. If other Tribunals require to be upgraded so does this

Tribunal. This example illustrates the disadvantages inherent in attempting to graft on to an institution designed and accustomed to serve quite different purposes, new jurisdictions for which it is intrinsically unsuited. By absorbing some only of the administrative appellate functions the problem of finding a satisfactory solution for the remainder is correspondingly increased. The majority is already faced with the dilemma of isolating transport charges from transport licensing generally. Anomalies of this kind should be avoided if at all possible.

9. The majority refer to two important corollaries of their proposal for an Administrative Division of the Supreme Court. These relate to the removal in certain cases of the need for the prerogative writs, and the creation of a right of appeal to the Court of Appeal on questions of law. Without going into details it should be stressed that precisely the same advantages would accrue from the establishment of an Administrative Court. The only difference is that since the jurisdiction of the Administrative Court would be more comprehensive than that of the Administrative Division of the Supreme Court, there would be correspondingly less need for the prerogative writs if the Administrative Court was established. They would not extend to any administrative tribunals over which the Administrative Court had appellate jurisdiction nor, of course to the Administrative Court itself. Since an appeal on all questions of law would lie to the Court of Appeal from the Administrative Court the possibility of conflicting decisions between the Supreme Court and the Administrative Court would, as I have earlier indicated, be satisfactorily resolved.

10. Another serious disadvantage in grafting these appellate functions on to the Supreme Court is that the opportunity is lost of creating an organic body which is capable of growth and development to meet the changing needs of society. The limitations inherent in the concept of an Administrative Division of the Supreme Court are readily apparent from the majority's Report. The proposal is at best a partial and limited solution to present problems whereas the Administrative Court could be moulded and developed to deal satisfactorily with a very much wider area of administrative justice. This is not the place to discuss future possibilities for an Administrative Court some of which are considered in my book and the K. J. Scott Memorial Lecture. Suffice it to say that the concept of a general Administrative Division of the Administrative Court which could adjudicate in an informal way over areas of friction in both central and local government is difficult to contemplate in the context of an Administrative Division of the Supreme Court.

11. For all the foregoing reasons the establishment of an Administrative Court is preferred to an Administrative Division of the Supreme Court.

12. I should make it clear that I am in general agreement with much of the Report of the majority. My dissent is directed almost entirely at paragraphs 35 to 40 inclusive (which relate to the proposal for an Administrative Division of the Supreme Court), and, of course, to those subsequent recommendations in respect to particular tribunals which would direct appeals to the proposed Administrative Division. In my view these, along with price control and transport charges, should all go to an Administrative Court.

[sgd.] G. S. Orr
(5. 1. 68)

Bibliography

B. Abel-Smith, and R. Stevens, *In Search of Justice* (1968).

Accident Compensation Corp., *The New Zealand Accident Compensation System* (1984).

Administrative Conference of the United States, Statement No. 12, *1987 ACUS Recs. and Rpts.* (1987).

Administrative Conference of the United States, 'Views of the Administrative Conference of the United States on the "Report on Selected Independent Regulatory Agencies" of the President's Advisory Council on Executive Organization', *Virginia L. Rev.*, 57 (1971), 927.

American Bar Association Section of Administrative Law, 'A Restatement of Scope-of-Review Doctrine', *Admin. L. Rev.*, 38 (1986), 233.

Automobile Association, *Road Atlas of New Zealand* (1974).

L. E. Beck, 'Specialized Courts and Judicial Review of Administrative Action: An Analysis for Future Consideration' (unpublished paper, 1987).

E. Bodenheimer, J. B. Oakley, and J. C. Love, *An Introduction to the Anglo-American Legal System* (1988).

Hon. S. G. Breyer, and R. B. Stewart, *Administrative Law and Regulatory Policy* (2nd edn. 1985).

L. N. Brown, and F. G. Garner, *French Administrative Law* (2nd edn. 1973).

L. N. Brown, and F. G. Jacobs, *The Court of Justice of The European Communities* (1977).

Bureau of the Census, *Statistical Abstract of the United States* (108th edn., 1988).

P. D. Carrington, D. J. Meador and M. Rosenberg, *Justice on Appeal* (1976).

R. A. Cass, 'Agency Review of Administrative Law Judges' Decisions', in Administrative Conference of the United States, *1983 Recs. and Rpts.* 115.

Rt. Hon. Sir R. Cooke, 'The Struggle for Simplicity in Administrative Law', in M. Taggart (ed.), *Judicial Review of Administrative Action in the 1980's* (1986).

Council on the Role of Courts, *The Role of Courts in American Society* (1984).

P. P. Craig, *Administrative Law* (1983).

S. J. Craig, 'Federal Income Tax and the Supreme Court: The Case Against a National Court of Tax Appeals', *Utah L. Rev.* (1983), 679.

R. C. Cramton, 'Administrative Procedure Reform: The Effects of S.1663 on the Conduct of Federal Rate Proceedings', *Admin. L. Rev.*, 16 (1964), 108.

D. P. Currie, and F. I. Goodman, 'Judicial Review of Federal Administrative Action: Quest for the Optimum Forum', *Colum. L. Rev.* 75 (1975), 1.

P. J. Dalton, and R. S. Dexter, *Constitutional Law* (1976).

K. C. Davis, *Administrative Law Treatise* (2nd edn. 1983).

—— *Discretionary Justice—A Preliminary Inquiry* (1969).

Rt. Hon. Sir R. Davison, 'The Role of the Courts in Modern Society', *Otago L. Rev.*, 4 (1979), 277.

Department of Statistics, *New Zealand Official Yearbook 1987–88* (92nd ann. edn. 1987).

S. A. de Smith, *Judicial Review of Administrative Action* (4th edn. 1980) (J. M. Evans, ed.).

The District Courts—An Interview with Sir Desmond Sullivan, Chief District Court Judge, NZLJ (1985) 88.

C. S. Diver, 'Statutory Interpretation in the Administrative State', *U. Pa. L. Rev.*, 133 (1985), 549.

C. Enright, *Judicial Review of Administrative Action* (1985).

S. Estreicher, and R. L. Revesz, 'Nonacquiescence by Federal Administrative Agencies', *Yale LJ* 98 (1989) 679.

R. H. Fallon, 'Of Legislative Courts, Administrative Agencies, and Article III', *Harv. L. Rev.*, 101 (1988), 915.

J. A. Farmer, *Tribunals and Government* (1974).

—— 'Administrative Division of the Supreme Court—An Experiment in Administrative Suicide', *NZLJ* (1969) 106.

Franks Committee Report [see Report of the Committee on Administrative Tribunals and Inquiries].

C. E. Freedeman, *The Conseil d'Etat in Modern France* (1961).

J. O. Freedman, 'Expertise and the Administrative Process', *Admin. L. Rev.*, 28 (1976), 363.

Hon. H. J. Friendly, *Federal Jurisdiction: A General View* (1973).

S. Galeotti, *The Judicial Control of Public Authorities in England and in Italy* (1954).

W. Gellhorn, 'Medical Malpractice Litigation (U.S.)—Medical Mishap Compensation (N.Z.)', *Cornell L. Rev.*, 73 (1988), 170.

W. Gellhorn, C. Byse, P. L. Strauss, T. Rakoff, and R. A. Schotland, *Administrative Law Cases and Comments* (8th edn. 1987).

E. N. Griswold, 'The Need for a Court of Tax Appeals', *Harv. L. Rev.*, 57 (1944), 1153.

M. H. Grunewald, 'Freedom of Information Act Dispute Resolution', *Admin. L. Rev.*, 40 (1988), 1.

Lord Hailsham, 'The Lord Chancellor and Judicial Independence', *Cambrian L. Rev.*, 11 (1980), 40.

L. L. Jaffe, *English and American Judges as Lawmakers* (1969).

Sir. K. J. Keith, 'Appeals from Administrative Tribunals—The Existing Judicial Experience', *Victoria U. of Wellington L. Rev.*, 5 (1969), 123.

M. Lambert, E. Lambert, R. Palenski, and K. Palenski (eds.), *Fourth Air New Zealand Almanac* (1986).

S. H. Legomsky, *Immigration and the Judiciary—Law and Politics in Britain and America* (1987).

— 'Forum Choices for the Review of Agency Adjudication: A Study of the Immigration Process', *Iowa L. Rev.*, 71 (1986), 1297.

R. M. Levin, 'Identifying Question of Law in Administrative Law', *Georgetown L. Rev.*, 74 (1985), 1.

P. J. Levinson, 'A Specialized Court for Immigration Hearings and Appeals', *Notre Dame Lawyer*, 56 (1981), 644.

J. S. Lubbers, 'Federal Agency Adjudications: Trying to See the Forest and the Trees', *Fed. Bar News & J.*, 31 (Nov. 1984), 383.

—— 'A Unified Corps of ALJs: A Proposal to Test the Idea at the Federal Level', *Judicature*, 65 (1981), 266.

H. T. Miller, 'A Court of Tax Appeals Revisited', *Yale LJ*, 85 (1975), 228.

E. Mureinik, 'The Application of Rules: Law or Fact', *LQ Rev.*, 98 (1982), 587.

N. L. Nathanson, 'The Administrative Court Proposal', *Virginia L. Rev.*, 57 (1971), 996.

J. F. Northey, 'The Administrative Division of the New Zealand Supreme Court: A Postscript', *Alberta L. Rev.*, 15 (1977), 186.

—— 'A Decade of Change in Administrative Law', *NZUL Rev.*, 6 (1974), 25.

—— 'An Administrative Division of the New Zealand Supreme Court—A Proposal for Law Reform', *Alberta L. Rev.*, 7 (1969), 62.

G. S. Orr, *An Administrative Court—Its Scope and Purpose* (K. J. Scott Memorial Lecture) (1965).

—— '*Report on Administrative Justice in New Zealand* (1964).

C. Palley, '*Decision Making in the Area of Public Order By English Courts*,' The Open University, D203, block II, pt. 3 (1976).

Rt. Hon. G. Palmer, *Unbridled Power—An Interpretation of New Zealand's Constitution and Government* (2nd edn. 1987).

V. W. Palmer and E. S. Bernstein, 'Establishing Federal Administrative Law Judges as an Independent Corps: The Heflin Bill', *Western New England L. Rev.*, 6 (1984), 673.

A. Paterson, 'First Report of the Public and Administrative Law Reform Committee (Judicature Amendment Act 1968)', *NZUL Rev.*, 3 (1969), 351.

R. J. Pierce, S. A. Shapiro, and P. R. Verkuil, *Administrative Law Process* (1985).

Hon. E. D. Re, 'Litigation Before the United States Court of International Trade', *N.Y.L. School L. Rev.*, 26 (1981), 437.

M. J. Remington, 'The Tribunaux Administratifs: Protectors of the French Citizen', *Tulane L. Rev.*, 51 (1976), 33.

Report of the Comm. on Administrative Tribunals and Enquiries [Franks Comm., U.K.], Cmnd. 218 (1957).

Report of the Commonwealth Administrative Review Comm., Parl. Paper No. 144 (1971) [Kerr Report].

Report, 'First Submissions of the New Zealand Law Society to the Royal Commission on the Courts', 1977 *N.Z.L.J.* 150 (1977).

Report of the Justice and Law Reform Committee on a White Paper on a Bill of Rights for New Zealand (1988).

Report, Law Comm'n, Rpt. No. 7, *The Structure of the Courts* (1989).

Report No. 3 of the Legislation Advisory Comm., *Administrative Tribunals* (1989).

Report, 'New Zealand Law Society Recs. to the Royal Comm'n on the Courts', *Lawtalk*, 52 (1977), 2.

Report (First) of the Public and Administrative Law Reform Comm. of New Zealand, *Appeals from Administrative Tribunals* (1968).

Report (Second) of the Public and Administrative Law Reform Comm. of New Zealand, *Appeals from Administrative Tribunals* (1969).

Report (Seventh) of the Public and Administrative Law Reform Comm. of New Zealand, *Administrative Tribunals Constitution, Procedure and Appeals* (1974).

Report (Twelfth) of the Public and Administrative Law Reform Comm. of New Zealand (1978).

Report (Fifteenth) of the Public and Administrative Law Reform Committee of New Zealand (1980).

Report, Royal Commission on the Courts [New Zealand] (1978).

Report, Royal Comm'n on the Electoral System, *Towards a Better Democracy* (1986).

M. A. Roberts, 'Proposed: A Specialized Statutory Immigration Court', *San Diego L. Rev.*, 18 (1980), 1.

G. O. Robinson, 'On Revamping the Independent Regulatory Agencies', *Virginia L. Rev.*, 57 (1971), 947.

—— E. Gellhorn, and H. H. Bruff, *The Administrative Process* (3rd edn. 1986).

Hon. P. W. Rodino, 'The Customs Courts Act of 1980', *NYL School L. Rev.*, 26 (1981), 459.
D. P. Ryan, *A Review of The Administrative Division of the High Court* (LL.M Thesis; Victoria University of Wellington Faculty of Law, 1980).
R. L. Saloschin, 'Proposal for An Independent Body', Remarks before the Federal Bar Assn., 8th Ann. Conf. on Openness in Government (16 March, 1982).
J. L. Sax, *Defending the Environment: A Strategy for Citizen Action* (1970).
H. G. Schermers, *Judicial Protection in The European Communities* (2nd edn. 1979).
B. Schwartz, *Administrative Law* (2nd edn. 1984).
Sir. W. J. Sim, and G. Cain, *The Practice of the High Court and Court of Appeal of New Zealand* (1987).
H. Street, *Justice in the Welfare State* (2nd edn. 1975).
M. Taggart, (ed.), *Judicial Review of Administrative Action in the 1980's* (1986).
H. W. R. Wade, *Administrative Law* (5th edn. 1982).
Hon. P. M. Wald, Speech to Amer. Bar Assn. Section of Admin. Law, *Admin. L. Rev.*, 40 (1988), 508.
P. C. Weiler, *In the Last Resort* (1974).
White Paper, *A Bill of Rights for New Zealand* (1985).
Rt. Hon. Sir R. Wild, 'The Administrative Division of the Supreme Court of New Zealand', *U. of Toronto LJ*, 22 (1972), 258.
W. A. Wilson, 'Questions of Degree', *Mod. L. Rev.*, 32 (1969), 361.
D. R. Woodward, and R. M. Levin, 'In Defense of Deference: Judicial Review of Agency Action', *Admin. L. Rev.*, 31 (1979), 329.
R. E. Wraith, and P. G. Hutchesson, *Administrative Tribunals* (1973).
C. W. Wright, *The Law of Federal Courts* (4th edn. 1983).
M. Zander, *The Law-Making Process* (1980).

Index

Printed in the United Kingdom
by Lightning Source UK Ltd.
129620UK00001B/29/A